Existential–
Humanistic Therapy

Theories of Psychotherapy Series

Existential–Humanistic Therapy
   Kirk J. Schneider and Orah T. Krug

Feminist Therapy
   Laura S. Brown

Relational–Cultural Therapy
   Judith V. Jordan

Theories of Psychotherapy Series
Jon Carlson and Matt Englar-Carlson, Series Editors

Existential–
Humanistic Therapy

Kirk J. Schneider and Orah T. Krug

American Psychological Association

Washington, DC

First Printing September 2009
Second Printing December 2010

Published by
American Psychological Association
750 First Street, NE
Washington, DC 20002
www.apa.org

To order
APA Order Department
P.O. Box 92984
Washington, DC 20090-2984
Tel: (800) 374-2721;
Direct: (202) 336-5510
Fax: (202) 336-5502;
TDD/TTY: (202) 336-6123
Online: www.apa.org/books/
E-mail: order@apa.org

In the U.K., Europe, Africa, and the
Middle East, copies may be ordered from
American Psychological Association
3 Henrietta Street
Covent Garden, London
WC2E 8LU England

Typeset in Minion by Shepherd, Inc., Dubuque, IA

Printer: United Book Press, Inc., Baltimore, MD
Cover Designer: Minker Design, Sarasota, FL
Technical/Production Editor: Emily Welsh

Cover art: *Lily Rising,* 2005, oil and mixed media on panel in craquelure frame, by Betsy Bauer.

The opinions and statements published are the responsibility of the authors, and such opinions and statements do not necessarily represent the policies of the American Psychological Association.

Library of Congress Cataloging-in-Publication Data

Schneider, Kirk J.
  Existential-humanistic therapy / Kirk J. Schneider and Orah T. Krug. -- 1st ed.
     p. cm.
  Includes bibliographical references and index.
  ISBN-13: 978-1-4338-0462-5 (alk. paper)
  ISBN-10: 1-4338-0462-X (alk. paper)
  1. Existential psychology. 2. Humanistic psychology. 3. Existential psychotherapy. I. Krug, Orah T. II. Title.
  BF204.5.S354 2010
  150.19'2--dc22
                          2009017973

British Library Cataloguing-in-Publication Data
A CIP record is available from the British Library.

Printed in the United States of America
First Edition

Contents

Series Preface

Some might argue that in the contemporary clinical practice of psychotherapy, evidence-based intervention and effective outcome have overshadowed theory in importance. Maybe. But, as the editors of this series, we don't propose to take up that controversy here. We do know that psychotherapists adopt and practice according to one theory or another because their experience, and decades of good evidence, suggests that having a sound theory of psychotherapy leads to greater therapeutic success. Still, the role of theory in the helping process can be hard to explain. This narrative about solving problems helps convey theory's importance:

> Aesop tells the fable of the sun and wind having a contest to decide who was the most powerful. From above the earth, they spotted a man walking down the street, and the wind said that he bet he could get his coat off. The sun agreed to the contest. The wind blew and the man held on tightly to his coat. The more the wind blew the tighter he held. The sun said it was his turn. He put all of his energy into creating warm sunshine and soon the man took off his coat.

What does a competition between the sun and wind to remove a man's coat have to do with theories of psychotherapy? We think this deceptively simple story highlights the importance of theory as the precursor to any effective intervention—and hence to a favorable outcome. Without a guiding theory, we might treat the symptom without understanding the role of the individual. Or we might create power conflicts with our clients and not understand that, at times, indirect means of helping (sunshine) are often as effective—if not more so—than direct ones (wind). In the absence of theory, we might lose track of the treatment rationale and instead get caught up in, for example, social correctness and not wanting to do something that looks too simple.

What exactly *is* theory? The *APA Dictionary of Psychology* defines theory as "a principle or body of interrelated principles that purports to explain or predict a number of interrelated phenomena." In psychotherapy, a theory is a set of principles used to explain human thought and behavior, including what causes people to change. In practice, a theory creates the goals of therapy and specifies how to pursue them. Haley (1997) noted that a theory of psychotherapy ought to be simple enough for the average therapist to understand, but comprehensive enough to account for a wide range of eventualities. Furthermore, a theory guides action toward successful outcomes while generating hope in both the therapist and client that recovery is possible.

Theory is the compass that allows psychotherapists to navigate the vast territory of clinical practice. In the same ways that navigational tools have been modified to adapt to advances in thinking and ever expanding territories to explore, theories of psychotherapy have changed over time. The different schools of theories are commonly referred to as *waves,* the first wave being psychodynamic theories (i.e., Adlerian, psychoanalytic), the second wave learning theories (i.e., behavioral, cognitive–behavioral), the third wave humanistic theories (person-centered, gestalt, existential), the fourth wave feminist and multicultural theories, and the fifth wave postmodern and constructivist theories. In many ways, these waves represent how psychotherapy has adapted and responded to changes in psychology, society, and epistemology as well as to changes in the nature of psychotherapy itself. Psychotherapy and the theories that guide it are dynamic and responsive. The wide variety of theories is also testament to the different ways in which the same human behavior can be conceptualized (Frew & Spiegler, 2008).

It is with these two concepts in mind—the central importance of theory and the natural evolution of theoretical thinking—that we developed the APA Theories of Psychotherapy Series. Both of us are thoroughly fascinated by theory and the range of complex ideas that drive each model. As university faculty members who teach courses on the theories of psychotherapy, we wanted to create learning materials that not only highlight the essence of the major theories for professionals and professionals in training but that also clearly bring the reader up to date on the current status of the models. Often in books on theory, the biography of the original theorist overshadows the evolution of the model. In contrast, our intent was to highlight the contemporary uses of the theories as well as their history and context.

As this project began, we faced two immediate decisions: which theories to address and who best to present them. We looked at graduate-level theories of psychotherapy courses to see which theories are being taught, and we explored popular scholarly books, articles, and conferences to determine which theories draw the most interest. We then developed a dream list of authors from among the best minds in contemporary theoretical practice. Each author is one of the leading proponents of that approach as well as a knowledgeable practitioner. We asked each author to review the core constructs of the theory, bring the theory into the modern sphere of clinical practice by looking at it through a context of evidence-based practice, and clearly illustrate how the theory looks in action.

There are 24 titles planned for the series. Each title can stand alone or can be put together with a few other titles to create materials for a course in psychotherapy theories. This option allows instructors to create a course featuring the approaches they believe are the most salient today. To support this end, APA Books has also developed a DVD for each of the approaches that demonstrates the theory in practice with a real client. Some of the DVDs show therapy over six sessions. Contact APA Books for a complete list of available DVD programs (http://www.apa.org/videos).

In this book, Drs. Kirk Schneider and Orah Krug show how existential–humanistic psychotherapy provides effective treatment in contemporary psychological practice. Drs. Schneider and Krug discuss numerous cases that will allow the reader to understand how this approach, rooted in philosophy, is also very practical. The authors highlight how the struggles of existence are often at the root of so much of our psychological suffering. Both authors use their extensive experience to provide a clear and concise delineation of the theory and practice of existential–humanistic therapy.

This is an approach that integrates not only existential and humanistic theories but also strategies and techniques from other contemporary approaches. As their case studies unfold, Drs. Schneider and Krug help the reader to gain familiarity with this theory, how it looks in practice, and how integration occurs.

Jon Carlson and Matt Englar-Carlson

REFERENCES

Frew, J., & Spiegler, M. (2008). *Contemporary psychotherapies for a diverse world.* Boston: Lahaska Press.

Haley, J. (1997). *Leaving home: The therapy of disturbed young people.* New York: Routledge.

Existential–
Humanistic Therapy

Introduction

Those with outward courage dare to die;
those with inward courage dare to live.

—Lao Tzu

How shall we live? What really matters to us? How can we pursue what really matters? As the quote that opens this text implies, this book is about the inward courage to live. Existential therapy is about helping people to reclaim and reown their lives. The basic principles of existential therapy are an expansion on the basic principles of all therapies that point beyond the conventional emphasis on external, mechanical change. For example, existential therapy expands on medical intervention by inviting reflection on the meaning of the intervention. Hence, if a withdrawn person uses Prozac to transform herself into a sociable person, the existential therapist might invite a dialogue with that person about the subjective meaning of that change. Is this the change that the person genuinely desires, or is this a change that is dictated by her peer group, culture, or employer, without essential reference to herself? And if this is not the change that the person deeply desires, what is that change? How can it be engaged? What is one's willingness to deal with its consequences? Or correspondingly, what if a depressed person uses a cognitive–behavioral strategy, such as rational reframing, to exhibit positive thoughts and behaviors? The existential therapist in such a case might question what "positive" means for that person. Does it mean a change that is enduring? Enriching? Emotionally and physically fulfilling? Or does it mean a change that is expedient? Convenient? Easy to assimilate? What are the consequences of such a change—a simpler but less reflective life? A "manageable" but jaded life? Existential therapists do not provide answers but help people to address questions.

The way in which existential therapists help people address these questions is also a unique part of our approach. It may seem from the preceding paragraph that we engage our clients primarily in an intellectual dialog but that is not the case. Instead we focus on the unfolding process in the living moment. We carefully attune to how our clients relate to themselves and to us, appropriately reflecting back aspects of themselves that are evident but unnoticed. We take note if our client is self-critical or indecisive. Does he relate to us in a dependent manner or in a detached and/or aloof manner? How does he occupy his personal space—with hesitation and constraint or with confidence and pluck?

Why do we focus our attention in this way? Because we assume that not only is our client before us, but so is her life: her wish to live and her awareness of death, her yearning for connection and her fear of rejection, her desire to change and her fear of the unknown. We believe that the meanings our client has made of her past experiences and life conditions are alive in the living moment, some more conscious than others, expressed in her body, her voice, her behavior, her values and attitudes. Everything she says or does reflects her relationship to herself, to others, and to her world in general. If we can deeply attune to her and help her be more present, she will more likely connect with what really matters to her and, as a result, revitalize her life.

These then are the mooring points, the enlarged frames, within which existential therapy operates. The question as to *who* or *what* is making a change—for example, the medication, the logical argument, the peer group, or the person him or herself— is pivotal from the existential standpoint, but so is the question of *how* change is pursued—that is, the "soup" or medium within which it is explored. Accompany us now as we enter full-throttle into the heart of existential practice—a practice that embraces the questions we have posed here: How shall you live? What really matters to you? How do you go about cultivating what really matters? These are issues that press upon each of us, but especially therapy clients who yearn for a full and meaningful life. This is a life beyond the expedient and mechanical, one that embraces the maximal spectrum of human possibilities from love to death, and fear to joy.

The focus of this book accordingly is on one particular expression of existential therapy, contemporary existential–humanistic therapy. Although myriad forms of existential therapy are discussed and applied throughout the world (e.g., see Cooper, 2003), existential–humanistic therapy has a distinctly American character (e.g., see Bugental, 1987; Burston, 2003; Cooper, 2003), and that is what we will largely confine ourselves to in this volume.

What do we mean by existential–humanistic therapy? Although we will expand on this concept throughout this text, here we provide a thumbnail sketch: Existential–humanistic therapy is an amalgam of European humanistic and existential philosophy and American humanistic psychology. Consolidated in the early 1960s, existential–humanistic therapy welds the European heritage of self-inquiry, struggle, and responsibility with the American tradition of spontaneity, optimism, and practicality. Brought together, existential–humanistic therapy forms a dynamic and timely stew.

In the chapters that follow, we will examine the history, theoretical framework, and practical application of existential–humanistic therapy as it is currently understood by a diverse and growing constituency. This constituency, comprised of both practitioners and clients, extends to a surprisingly broad cultural and diagnostic arena, and it is increasingly challenging stereotypes. One stereotype is that existential–humanistic practice is a "high-brow" form of philosophy, relevant only to cultural elites. Another stereotype is that existential–humanistic practice is hyper-individualistic and does not validate connections *between* people. Still another presumption and misnomer is that existential–humanistic psychotherapy is capricious and undisciplined. While these stereotypes might seem to have some legitimacy, particularly in the context of certain delimited influences from the human potential movement of the 1960s (Moss, 2001), they ring increasingly hollow (Burston, 2003; O'Hara, 2001; Schneider, 2008).

As we shall see, today's existential–humanistic therapy is applicable to a wide array of settings, diagnostic populations, and ethnicities (see especially chapter 4), and because the personal and interpersonal context is at the core of existential–humanistic training, it is becoming an increasing influence on the therapeutic profession as a whole (Schneider, 2008; Wampold, 2008).

"Expanded horizons notwithstanding," however, as Mendelowitz and Schneider (2008) put it in a recent chapter, "contemporary existential psychology shares with its predecessors this bedrock value: the uncanny core to be found at the heart of existence and the spirit of inquiry that resides at the deepest levels of consciousness" (p. 303). We shall now turn to this "uncanny core" and its legacy of literary, philosophical, and psychological depth.

2

History

Existential–humanistic theory is rooted in the deepest recesses of recorded time. All who addressed the question of what it means to be fully and subjectively alive have partaken in the existential–humanistic quest. Existentialism derives from the Latin root *ex-sistere*, which literally means to "stand forth" or to "become" (May, 1958a, p. 12), whereas humanism originates in the ancient Greek tradition of "knowing thyself" (Grondin, 1995, p. 112). Therefore, existential humanism can be understood as a process of becoming and knowing oneself.

In the early 1960s, American humanistic psychology drew on both humanism and existentialism to bring a new dimension to psychology. This dimension opposed what it viewed as reductionistic trends in psychoanalysis and behaviorism and emphasized such qualities as choice, spontaneity of expression, and transcendence. But it also emphasized, thanks mainly to its philosophical wing, the existential accents on death, poignancy, and human limitation (Burston, 2003; May, 1958a). To some extent, these

Portions of the following three chapters have been excerpted and/or adapted from "Existential–Humanistic Psychotherapies," by Kirk Schneider, 2003, in A. Gurman & S. Messer (Eds.), *Essential Psychotherapies* (2nd ed., pp. 149–181), New York: Guilford Press. Copyright 2003 by Guilford Press.

latter emphases set the existential dimension apart from other humanistic-oriented purviews, such as those formulated by Rogers (1951) and Perls (1971) on the one hand and elements of the transpersonal movement on the other (May, 1981; Mendelowitz & Schneider, 2008). Those departures will be explored in more detail; for now, it is enough to say that today, existential humanism is a distinctly American amalgam that combines existential accents on human limitation with humanistic accents on human possibility. This combination creates a paradoxical unity of complementary opposites. Existential–humanistic therapy consequently embraces three values: freedom (to become within the givens of human limitation), experiential reflection (to grapple with the challenges to what one becomes), and responsibility (to act on or respond to what one becomes). To put it another way, contemporary existential–humanistic therapy stresses (1) the "whole-bodied" (that is, cognitive–affective–kinesthetic) capacity to choose, within limits, who one will become; (2) the whole-bodied capacity to discern the meaning of those choices; and (3) the whole-bodied capacity to act on or express the choices made.

Based on these values, existential–humanistic therapy has developed a methodology grounded in the assumption that fundamental change occurs, not merely through intellectual or behavioral reprogramming, but through experiential or "whole-bodied" reawakening. To illustrate this point, take the case of Hamilton, who, as we shall see later in this volume, suffered from a fear of heights. Although Hamilton learned to suppress this fear through conditioning techniques, it wasn't until he was able to be fully and experientially present to his fear that he learned to work through and transform it.

Consequently, the key to the existential–humanistic approach is an emphasis on whole-bodied encounter. This type of approach is critical in our view, particularly as clients develop what we call *intentionality*, or the capacity to (re)claim their lives.

ORIGINS

Although existential humanism has its roots in Socratic, Renaissance, Romantic, and even Asiatic sources, as depicted in the quote to start this volume (Moss, 2001; Schneider, 1998a; Taylor, 1999), it was not until the mid-19th century that existential philosophy, as such, was formalized. With the advent of Soren Kierkegaard's (1844/1944) *Concept of Dread*, a new era had dawned in which freedom, experiential reflection, and responsibility played an increasingly pivotal philosophical and therapeutic role. In Kierkegaard's thesis, freedom emerges from crisis, and crisis from intellectual, emotional, or physical imprisonment. In Kierkegaard's time, this imprisonment often took the form of robotic adherence to the Catholic Church or to objectifying trends in science. But it could be any limiting experience. Kierkegaard called these limiting experiences the points at which "angst" or anxiety "educate":

> Whoever is educated by anxiety is educated by possibility, and only he who is educated by possibility is educated according to his infinitude. Therefore possibility is the weightiest of all categories . . . this possibility is commonly regarded as the possibility of happiness, fortune, etc. But this is not possibility . . . No, in possibility all things are equally possible, and whoever has truly been brought up by possibility has grasped the terrible as well as the joyful. So . . . such a person graduates from the school of possibility, and he knows better than a child knows his ABC's that he can demand absolutely nothing of life and that the terrible, perdition, and annihilation live next door to every man . . . (p. 156)

Kierkegaard was nothing if not complex and paradoxical. In one of the most damning oppositions to social objectification and doctrinaire living ever waged, Kierkegaard called for a complete transformation of values. We must move, Kierkegaard exclaimed, from a mechanized or externalized life to one that is centered in the subject and that struggles for the truth of the subject. It is only through facing and grappling with our *selves,* he elaborated, that consciousness can expand, deepen, and seek its vibrant potential.

Writing at about the same time, but with an even feistier style, Friedrich Nietzsche (1844–1900), traced the devitalization of conventional culture to the dominance of Apollonian (or rationalist–linear living) over Dionysian (or non-rationalist–spontaneous) living. Although these strains were in tension—in Nietzsche's time, as in the time of the ancient Greeks who formulated them—Nietzsche foresaw the era when Apollonian technocracy would overshadow and level all in its path. To remedy this situation, and to restore the Dionysian spirit, Nietzsche (1889/1982) called for a Dionysian-Apollonian rapprochement. This rapprochement would "afford" people "the whole range and wealth of being natural," but also, and in concert with the latter, the capacity for being "strong, highly educated," and "self-controlled" (p. 554).

The next major revolution in existential–humanistic psychology and philosophy occurred in the early 20th century, with the advent of behaviorism and psychoanalysis. While behaviorism, championed by such advocates as John Watson, stressed the mechanistic and overt aspects of human functioning, psychoanalysis, spearheaded by Freud and his followers, promoted covert intrapsychic determinism. In neither case, existential humanists contended, was the human psyche illuminated in its radiant and enigmatic fullness, its liberating and yet vulnerable starkness, and so they rebelled. Among these rebellions were the far-ranging meditations of William James (1902/1936) on spirituality, Otto Rank (1936) on the fear of life and fear of death, C. G. Jung (1966) on mythology, and Henry Murray (Murray et al., 1938) on creativity. But while this group drew tangentially from existential–humanistic philosophy, another group of mainly former Freudians drew directly on the existential–humanistic lineage. Ludwig Binswanger (1958) and Medard Boss (1963), for example, based their psychiatric practices on the existential and phenomenological philosophy of Martin Heidegger (1962) and Edmund Husserl (1913/1962). Expanding on Kierkegaard's emphasis on the subjective, Heidegger developed a philosophy of being. By being, Heidegger meant neither self-enclosed individualism nor deterministic realism, but a "lived" amalgam of the two he termed "being-in-the-world." Being-in-the-world is Heidegger's attempt to illustrate that our Western tradition of separating inner from outer, or subjective from objective, is misleading and that, from the standpoint of experience, there is no clear way to separate them. In a phrase, we are both separate subjective selves *and* related to the external world, according to Heidegger. To develop his thesis, Heidegger drew on the method and practices of phenomenology, originated by his mentor, Edmund Husserl. According to Husserl (1913/1962), the chief task of phenomenology is to apprehend human experience in its living reality—that is, in its full subjective and intersubjective context (see also Churchill & Wertz, 2001; Giorgi, 1970).

By the 1960s, existential–humanistic (E–H) psychotherapy—under the banner of its umbrella movement, humanistic psychology—evolved into a mature and recognized perspective, but it was also a varied perspective. While most E–H practitioners stressed freedom, experiential reflection, and responsibility, they did so with varying degrees of intensity. There were times, for example, such as in the aftermath of World War II and during the flowering of the human potential movement of the 1960s, when existential freedom may have been stressed to the neglect of responsibility (e.g., see May, 1969, 1981; Merleau-Ponty, 1962; Yalom, 1980); or other times when responsibility was accented to the detriment of freedom (Rowan, 2001); or experiential reflection to the neglect of responsibility (Spinelli, 2001).

To further complicate matters, with the advent of Rollo May's (1958) edited book, *Existence*, which "imported" existential psychology to America, the broad outlines of E–H practice philosophy collapsed into two distinct camps, one emphasizing the cultural traditions of continental Europe and the other the historical influences of the United States. While the former, "existential–analytic" camp evolved a comparatively restrained, verbal style, the latter "existential–humanistic" camp developed a comparatively expansive, experiential style. For example, whereas an existential–analytic practitioner might comment on a client's upbeat story (thus staying "right with" the client's manifest intentions), an existential–humanistic practitioner might take a calculated risk to invite the client to notice how he's hunched over as he tells his story (thus expanding upon the client's manifest intentions). These respective styles and the controversies they generate persist today (see Burston, 2003; Cooper, 2003; and Schneider, Bugental, & Pierson, 2001, for elaboration).

CONTEMPORARY APPROACH: EVOLUTION TO PRESENT

Despite and perhaps in light of these controversies, today's E–H practitioners have an advantage over those of their predecessors—hindsight. With such hindsight, many contemporary E–H therapists are wary of one-sided formulations, be they of the existential–humanistic variety or those with which E–H practitioners traditionally differ. Contemporary E–H practitioners, moreover, tend to value a pluralistic understanding of human nature, psychotherapeutic integration, and complementariness among therapeutic approaches. They tend to see the intrapsychic aspects of therapy on a par with those of intersubjectivity, the social and cultural implications of their work on a level with individual transformation, and the intellectual and philosophical bases of practice on a plane with those of emotion and spirit. The contemporary E–H practitioner, moreover, does not shy away from programmatic or even biological interventions, as those may be appropriate (Schneider, 1995, 2008).

While the field of E–H therapy has not traditionally included many female practitioners, this situation is changing. E–H therapy now embraces a range of female practitioners who influence its focus and tone (Brown, 2008; Comas-Diaz, 2008; Fosha, 2008; Krug, 2009; Monheit, 2008; Serlin, 2008; Sterling, 2001). Until recently, with the exception of one of its founders, Charlotte Buhler, very few female voices had been heard expressing their interpretations of E–H therapy. The advent of this substantial group of female voices in itself has been a corrective by providing an intrinsically feminine perspective of E–H therapy as a counterpoint to the heretofore almost exclusively male one.

This breadth of outlook, coupled with a more diverse group of practitioners, has widened the existential–humanistic client base. Less and less is E–H practice confined to the rarified environs of its psychoanalytic forebears or to upper class elites; it is opening out to the world within which most of us dwell (O'Hara, 2001; Pierson & Sharp, 2001). Put another way, the E–H *attitude* can be seen in a variety of practice settings, including drug counseling (Ballinger, Matano, & Amantea, 2008), therapy with war veterans (Decker, 2007), therapy with minorities (Alsup, 2008;

Rice, 2008; Vontress & Epp, 2001), gay and lesbian counseling (Brown, 2008; Monheit, 2008), therapy with psychotic clientele (Dorman, 2008; Mosher, 2001; Thompson, 1995), emancipatory practices with groups (E. Bugental, 2008; Lerner, 2000; Lyons, 2001; Montuori & Purser, 2001; O'Hara, 2001), cognitive–behavioral interventions with anxious and phobic clients (Bunting & Hayes, 2008; Wolfe, 2008), psychodynamic mediations with spiritually and religiously distressed clients (Hoffman, 2008), and neurobiological and experiential interventions with sufferers of attachment disorder (Fosha, 2008).

Yet in spite of their expanded vision, contemporary E–H practitioners still share a core value with their predecessors—the personal or intimate search process that is at the crux of depth practice. By "depth practice," we mean practice that is intensive, exploratory, and embodied. We also mean the provision of four basic stances or conditions. These stances, which will be elaborated in the next chapter, are (1) the cultivation of therapeutic presence, (2) the activation of presence through struggle, (3) the working through of resistance (or protections), and (4) the coalescence of meaning and awe.

(For additional references to the existential–humanistic philosophical heritage, see also Barrett, 1958; Becker, 1973; Buber, 1937/1970; Camus, 1955; deBeauvior, 1948; Friedman, 1991a; Marcel, 1956; Sartre, 1956; and Tillich, 1952. For additional references to the psychological heritage of existential humanism, see Bugental, 1965; Frankl, 1963; May, 1983; Moustakas, 1972; Rogers, 1951; Schneider & May, 1995; Wheelis, 1958; and Yalom, 1980.)

3

Theory

GOALS OF THE APPROACH

Freedom Within Limits

The aim of existential–humanistic (E–H) therapy is to "set clients free" (May, 1981, p. 19). Freedom is understood as the capacity for choice within the natural and self-imposed limits of living (Schneider, 2008). The natural limits of living refer to the inherent limitations of birth, heredity, age, etc., and the realities of living—often referred to as "the givens of existence"—such as death, separateness, and uncertainty. Self-imposed limits are the boundaries established by humans, such as culture, language, and lifestyle.

The freedom to do or to act is probably the clearest freedom we possess. The freedom to be or to adopt attitudes toward situations is a less clear but even more fundamental freedom (May, 1981). Freedom to do is generally associated with external, physical decisions, whereas freedom to be is associated with internal, cognitive, and emotional stances. Within these freedoms we have a great capacity to create meaning in our lives—to conceptualize, imagine, invent, communicate, and physically and psychologically enlarge our worlds (Yalom, 1980). We also have the capacity to separate from others, to transcend our past, and to become distinct, unique, and heroic (Becker, 1973). Conversely, we can choose to restrain ourselves, to become passive, and to give ourselves over to others (May, 1981; Rank, 1936). We can choose to be a part of others or apart from others, a part of our possibilities or apart from our possibilities (Bugental & Kleiner, 1993).

Acknowledge Freedom's Limitations

Notwithstanding the vast possibilities, there are great limitations on all these freedoms. We can only do and be so much. Whatever we choose implies a relinquishment of something else (Bugental, 1987, p. 230). If we devote ourselves to scholarship, we relinquish a degree of athleticism. If we engage in wealth accumulation, we lessen our opportunities for spiritual pursuits. Moreover, every freedom has its price. If one stands out in a crowd, one becomes a larger target for criticism; if one acquires responsibility, one courts guilt; if one isolates oneself, one loses community; if one merges and fuses with others, one loses individuality, and so on (Becker, 1973; May, 1981). Finally, every freedom has its counterpart in destiny. May (1981) defines four kinds of destiny, or "givens" beyond our control: cosmic, genetic, cultural, and circumstantial. Cosmic destiny embraces the limitations of nature (e.g., earthquakes, climatic shifts); genetic destiny entails physiological dispositions (e.g., life span, temperament); cultural destiny addresses preconceived social patterns (e.g., language, birthrights); and circumstantial destiny pertains to sudden situational developments (e.g., oil spills, job layoffs). In short, our vast potentialities are matched by crushing vulnerabilities. We are semiaware, semicapable, in a world of dazzling incomprehensibility.

How, then, shall we deal with these clashing realities according to existential theorists, and what happens when we do not? Let us consider the latter first. The failure to acknowledge our freedom, according to existential theorists, results in the dysfunctional identification with limits, or repressed living (May, 1981). This dysfunctional identification forfeits the capacity to enliven, embolden, and enlarge one's perspective. The reticent wallflower, the pedantic bureaucrat, the paranoid reactionary, and the robotic conformist are illustrations of this polarity. The failure to acknowledge our limits, on the other hand, results in the sacrifice of our ability to discipline, discern, and prioritize life's chances (May, 1981). The aimless dabbler, the impulsive con man, the unbowed hedonist, and the power-hungry elitist exemplify this polarity.

Integrate Freedom and Limitation

The great question, of course, is how to help clients become emancipated from their polarized conditions and "experience their possibilities" as they engage their destinies (May, 1981, p. 20). Put another way, how do we help clients to *integrate* freedom and limits? This question strikes at the heart of another existential problem—that of identity. Whereas reprogramming clients' behaviors or helping them to understand the genesis of their polarized conditions leads to partially rejuvenated identities, for existential theorists, *experiential* encounters with these conditions are the great underappreciated complements to the aforementioned change processes (Schneider, 2007, 2008). The E–H practitioner believes that if life-limiting patterns are experienced in the present, then clients will be more willing and able to choose life-affirming patterns in the future. Put another way, the path to greater freedom is paradoxically found through an encounter with the ways in which we are bound (Krug, 2009).

The experiential modality for existential theorists embraces four basic dimensions: the immediate, the kinesthetic, the affective, and the profound or cosmic (Schneider, 2008). The road to a fuller, more vital identity, in other words, is to help clients experience their polarized conditions, to assist them to "embody" those conditions and their underlying fears and anxieties, and to help them attune, at the deepest levels, to the implications of what has been discovered. In so doing, E–H therapists help clients to respond to, as opposed to react against, panic-filled material. This work typically results in clients experiencing their polarized conditions as restrictive or self-limiting. Consequently, it not only allows clients to understand their part in the construction of their restrictive patterns, it also helps them accept the givens of existence that may have been avoided, denied, or repressed. However, for the E–H practitioner, responsibility assumption is not sufficient. It is simply preparatory for substantive change evidenced when clients choose more life-affirming patterns for themselves and with others. (This process of affirming one's being by acknowledging one's limitations is illustrated by the short case of Mimi in chapter 4 who must first relinquish her "sense of specialness" so she can embrace more life-affirming patterns.) The net result, according to existential theorists, is an expanded sense of self, specifically an enhanced capacity for intimacy, meaning, and spiritual connection in one's life (Bugental, 1978; May, 1981).

An Illustration of This Process

The classic case of Mercedes, by Rollo May (1972), further illustrates this standpoint. Mercedes lived much of her life in subordination to others. Her stepfather was a pimp and her mother a prostitute. Mercedes herself was coerced into prostitution to enable the family to subsist. Yet Mercedes bristled at her subservient position. She harbored tremendous resentment toward her "clientele" and even more toward her "caretakers." She was frequently depressed, impaired in her love life, and unable to carry her pregnancies with her husband to full term. May utilized many approaches to help Mercedes confront and integrate her rage, which in his view portended her freedom. These efforts, however, invariably failed to spark her, until one day when he encountered her experientially. Instead of encouraging *her* to acknowledge her resentment, *he* acknowledged it for her. *He* vented his fury on her stepfather; *he* unleashed his indignation toward her mother; and *he* embodied the bitterness she had harbored. In turn, Mercedes was finally able to affirm and express these qualities— directly and bodily—in herself. The upshot, according to May, is that Mercedes integrated her freedom: She quit prostitution, revived her marriage, and carried her pregnancy to term.

Varied Interpretations of Experiential Encounter

The experiential mode is diversely interpreted by existential theorists. For example, Yalom (1980) appears to stress the immediate and affective elements of his interpersonal therapeutic contacts, but he refers little to kinesthetic components. Bugental (1987) stresses kinesthetic elements of his encounters—illuminating what is "implicitly present but unregarded" (Bugental, 1999, p. 25)—but places lesser emphasis on interpersonal implications of those elements (Krug, 2009). Tillich (1952) and Friedman (1995) accent the interpersonal dimension of therapeutic experiencing but convey little about the kinesthetic aspect.

There are also differences among existential theorists regarding verbal and nonverbal channels of communication. May (1983), Yalom (1980), and Friedman (1995), for example, rely relatively heavily on verbal interventions, whereas Bugental (1987), Gendlin (1996), and Laing (1967) draw upon comparatively nonverbal forms of mediation.

Finally, there are differences among existential theorists with regard to philosophical implications of therapeutic experiencing. Although most existential theorists agree that clients need to confront the underlying givens (or ultimate concerns) of human existence during the course of a typical therapy, the nature and specificity of these givens varies. Whereas Yalom (1980), for example, focuses on the need for clients to experientially confront death, freedom, isolation, or meaninglessness, Bugental provides a more elaborate schema: the need for clients to confront embodiment–change, finitude–contingency, action–responsibility, choice–relinquishment, separation–apartness, or relation–being a part of (Bugental & Kleiner, 1993). And whereas May (1981) unites these positions with his notion of freedom and destiny (or limitation), as previously suggested, there is only a vague explication of this synthesis in his work.

A Central Concern: The Present Moment

Despite these differences, each theorist shares a central concern—namely, how is this client in this moment coping with his or her awareness of being alive? The E–H theorists address this concern by focusing more on the implicit—moment to moment—processes in therapy than on explicit content. E–H theorists take an ahistorical approach; that is, the past is integral only insofar as it is alive, within the person, in the present moment. Moreover, E–H therapists seek to understand a person as a human being in the world, related to his or her physical, personal, and social worlds. It is assumed that a person is not simply a collection of drives and behavior patterns within an encapsulated self. It is further assumed that each person is more than the sum of his or her parts and that each person constructs a particular world from unique perceptions of the world. Finally, the E–H therapist assumes, as May (1983) suggests, that "the person and his world are a unitary, structural whole . . . two poles, self and world, are always dialectically related" (p. 122).

Consequently, the E–H theorist takes a step back from examining a person's drives and specific behavior patterns; with a wider scope, she or he understands these in the context of a person's relation to existence (May, 1958a, 1958b; Merleau-Ponty, 1962). These relations, which manifest as *structures*, are not abstract but actual, and though they may be obscured from conscious awareness, they are nevertheless evident (though perhaps implied) in the present moment. They express themselves through words spoken, and not through bodily gestures, vocal tones, dreams, and behavior patterns.

The Cultivation of Presence

The existential therapist aims to know the person who comes for therapy at this "structural" level. As May (1958b) states, "The grasping of the being of the other person occurs on a quite different level from our knowledge of specific things about him" (p. 38). In order to "grasp the being" of the client, and consequently help the client "grasp her being," the therapist must bring a full and genuine presence to the therapeutic encounter. The Latin root for *presence* is *prae* (before) + *esse* (to be); thus, *presence* means "to be before." Consequently, presence in a therapeutic setting can be understood as the capacity "to be before" or to be with one's being and/or "to be before" or to be with another human being.

Presence involves aspects of awareness, acceptance, availability, and expressiveness in both therapist and client. Presence implies that the encounter is real. For Martin Buber (1970), it means that the person who is before one has ceased being an "it" and has become a "thou"; it means that we are all humans who include each other in each other's recognition. Indeed, as Gabriel Marcel (1951) suggests, intersubjective presence begins with *"we are"* as opposed to *"I think."* If one can be truly present with another, then a genuine encounter has occurred.

Even with this emphasis on presence, E–H theorists recognize the influence of the past in their present-centered encounters. They acknowledge, for example, the power of developmental deficits to impact therapeutic processes (Schneider, 2008; Yalom, 1980). However, the bases of those deficits and the contexts within which they are addressed differ significantly from those advanced by more conventional standpoints. For example, whereas psychoanalytically oriented theorists tend to view ruptures in early interpersonal relationships as the bases for developmental deficits, E–H-oriented theorists take a wider view. This view acknowledges those early ruptures but goes beyond them to embrace the fuller experience of rupture or estrangement before being itself (May, 1981; Schneider, 2008; Yalom, 1980). Put another way, whereas psychoanalytic theorists tend to focus on isolable family or physiological factors in the etiology of suffering, E–H theorists tend to home in on dimensions that are purported to underlie such factors, such as the experience of life's vastness, the terror of dissolving before, or, on the other hand, exploding into life's vastness and the struggle with the enigma of death (Becker, 1973; Schneider, 1993, 1999a, 2008; Yalom, 1980).

Given this background, it may now be clearer why E–H theorists focus on here-and-now *experiences* of the past (as manifested in body posture, vocal tone, etc.) over discussions *about* the past. Whereas discussions can help clients to assimilate a specifiable event, such as an abuse memory, experiential awareness can help clients to assimilate the life stance, such as the sense of dissolution that both echoes and transcends the event.

For E–H theorists, accordingly, the deepest roots of trauma cannot simply be talked about or explained away; they must be rediscovered, felt, and lived through (Bugental, 1987; Krug, 2009; Schneider, 2008).

Four Core Aims

To sum, E–H theorists share four core aims: (a) to help clients to become more present to themselves and others; (b) to help them experience the ways in which they both mobilize and block themselves from fuller presence;

(c) to help them take responsibility for the construction of their current lives; and (d) to help them choose or actualize ways of being in their outside lives based on facing, not avoiding, the existential givens such as finiteness, ambiguity, and anxiety.

KEY CONCEPTS

Sense of Self

E–H psychology assumes that one does not experience a personality; one lives an experience. Moreover, E–H psychology assumes that lived experience is the basis on which one forms or creates a sense of self (May, 1975). E–H theorists' understanding of identity formation, or the "I am" experience, has been significantly influenced by May's perspective on human experience. His perspective focuses on awareness as an essence of being that has two dimensions. The first dimension is the fact of awareness: Every person is aware that she or he exists and consequently copes in various ways with this awareness. This is understood as the "existential predicament" and has been a major focus of existential philosophy and psychology (see Camus, 1955; Marcel, 1956; Sartre, 1956; May, 1975, 1981).

The second dimension focuses on how a person is aware and refers to the foundational structure of human experience—namely how anxiety, which stems from awareness of existence, drives a person to create meaning through an ongoing dialectical process between the subjective and objective poles of reality. May (1975) asserts that this dialectical process of meaning making, which he calls "passion for form," is the essence of genuine creativity. May acknowledges that his principle of human experience is similar to the ideas of several great philosophers, one of whom is Alfred N. Whitehead.

Whitehead's philosophy is part of a philosophical tradition going back to Heraclitus that focuses on process. Reality is not an assortment of material things, which is the Aristotelian notion, but one of process. Nature is a process not a thing. A river is not a thing but a continuing flow. Therefore, human beings, being a part of nature, are understood as a matter of process, of activity, of change (Rescher, 2000).

In Whitehead's ontology every organism or "occasion of experience" is "a dipolar unity . . . that enfolds . . . the past . . . into the present . . . and orients the organism toward the future in a 'creative advance'" (deQuincy, 2002, p. 174). A significant aspect of the structure of experience is that the past is always flowing into the present moment. Another significant aspect is the ongoing shaping of experience into a pattern from the "welter of material" from the past and from the external world. Whitehead argues that a person is never simply aware of bare existence or thought. Awareness is a person's subjective reaction to his or her environment derived from a shaping of a welter of emotions, thoughts, hopes, fears, and valuations into a consistent pattern of feelings. According to Whitehead, this shaping results in a sense of unity or "I am." May (1975) specifically correlates his conceptualization of "passion for form" and its relationship to the formation of a sense of self or identity to Whitehead's "process of shaping" and the resulting "sense of unity":

> What I am calling passion for form is, if I understand Whitehead aright, a central aspect of what he is describing as the experience of identity. I am able to shape feelings, sensibilities, enjoyments, and hopes into a pattern that makes me aware of myself as a man or woman. But I cannot shape them into a pattern as a purely subjective act. I can do it only as I am related to the immediate objective world in which I live. (p. 135)

Whitehead's process perspective provides May, and existential psychotherapy, with a sound philosophical position from which to explain how a sense of identity is created. Identity is created not as a purely subjective act but only as a dialectical process with the objective world. By understanding the "I am" experience as an ongoing dialectical process between subjective and objective poles, E–H theorists and practitioners have a more complex understanding of how a sense of self or identity is created and maintained. This understanding can be like a roadmap for therapists, helping them to see more clearly in the living moment the ways in which their clients are forming their worlds. The roadmap also elucidates the significant role the therapist plays in helping a client reconstitute his or her world. Finally, the roadmap confirms in a concrete way a basic assumption of existential therapy, which is that human beings have the potential to grow and re-create themselves through ongoing creative practices.

Patterns of Psychological Health

As previously noted, the notion of psychological health can have a static, culturally normative quality that may not reflect the lived experience of distinctive individuals (see Becker, 1973; Fromm, 1941; Wheelis, 1958). Nevertheless, there are patterns within these lived experiences (characterological structures) that existential humanists have carefully described phenomenologically. Let us consider a sampling.

May: Freedom and Destiny

The E–H understanding of functionality, as noted earlier, rests on three interdependent dimensions: freedom, experiential reflection, and the assumption of responsibility. While E–H theorists almost invariably highlight all three of these dimensions, they do so in unique and variegated ways. For example, Rollo May (1981) gives primary attention to freedom and that which he terms "destiny." By freedom, May means the capacity to choose within the natural and self-imposed (e.g., cultural) limits of living. Freedom also implies responsibility, for, as he suggests, if we are conferred the power to choose, is it not incumbent upon us to exercise that power?

It is the dynamic encounter with the clashing polarities of freedom and destiny, then, that gives life meaning (May, 1981). Only through struggle, May emphasizes, can freedom and destiny, capabilities and limits, be illuminated in their fullness, substantively explored, and meaningfully transformed.

Bugental: The Embodied yet Changing Self

The polarities of freedom and destiny or limitation, and the challenge to respond to these polarities, are central to leading E–H theorists' conceptions of psychological health. James Bugental (Bugental & Sterling, 1995), for example, draws on a similar dialectic with his emphasis on the self as embodied, yet changing; choiceful, yet finite; isolated, yet related. We are ever in the process of change, according to Bugental (consider, also, the ancient Greek philosopher Heraclitus), no matter how we choose to conceive it. Our challenge, Bugental elaborates, is to face that change, sort through its manifold features, and etch out of it a meaningful and action-oriented response.

Yalom: Four "Givens" of Existence

Irvin Yalom (1980) conceives of four "givens" of human existence—death, freedom, isolation, and meaninglessness. Depending on how we confront these givens, Yalom elaborates, we confront the design and quality of our lives. To the extent that we confront death, for example, we also encounter the urgency, intensity, and seriousness that death arouses. To the extent that we confront isolation, we also contact and become aware of our needs for relation or their opposite, solitude. For Yalom, the composition of a life is directly proportional to the composition and array of one's relationship to givens and the priorities one sets to integrate, explore, or coexist with those givens.

Greening: The Givens as Dimensions or Dialectics

An elaboration of Yalom's work by Greening (1992) understands the givens as existential dimensions or dialectics (e.g., life and death, freedom and determinism, meaning and absurdity, relatedness and separateness). Greening suggests that as paradoxical dialectics, each given challenges us to respond, and we do so by embracing each in one of three ways: (a) through a simplistic overemphasis on the positive aspects, (b) through a simplistic overemphasis on the negative aspects, and (c) through a confrontation, creative response, and transcendence of the dialectic. According to Greening, psychological health or maturity, from an existential perspective, is the capacity to accept and creatively respond to all four existential dialectics.

Let us now explore how each of the givens is a challenge to respond:

1. Life (and death) challenges us to respond because of our awareness that we are alive and that we will die. One response is an overemphasis on aliveness, optimism, and death denial, as in death-defying activities. Another response is to be pessimistic, obsessed with dying, accident prone, and neglectful of health. Finally, a third response

is to confront the dialectic and engage fully in the present moment knowing, as Camus observed, that we have no future—we choose life knowing we will die.

2. Meaning (and absurdity) challenges us because we are limited in our capacity to be conscious and make meaning. One response is an overemphasis on rational or intuitive thought or on blind faith, as in true believers addicted to cults, ideologies, or gurus. Another response is an anti-intellectual or a militantly atheistic or nihilistic stance—the result is a flight to action through drugs or death to escape consciousness. A third and more creative response is to face the absurdity and, in spite of it, to make satisfying personal meanings—to choose and act while remaining open to revision.

3. Freedom (and determinism) challenges us because we are finitely free. One response is an assertion of boundless freedom, regardless of the impact on others. Another response is an abdication of freedom resulting in self-enslavement, codependency, and substance abuse, for example. A third and more creative response is an exploration of possibilities with awareness of the interpersonal and physical context.

4. Community (and aloneness) challenges us because we are social beings, conceived, born, and raised in relationships. At the same time, we are separate physical and psychological entities. One response is a denial of isolation, over-involvment in organizations, selfless service, and enmeshed relationships. Another response is resignation to loneliness or a rejection of people, snobbishness, or self-effacement to avoid the risk of rejection. A third and more creative response is a willingness to engage authentically with another in a world where one may likely get treated as an object—to reach out to another in spite of the possibility of rejection.

Schneider: The Constrictive/Expansive Continuum and the EI Approach

Schneider (1999a, 2008) has elaborated a constrictive/expansive continuum of conscious and subconscious personality functioning. This continuum is identified as a capacity that is freeing, yet limited. We have a vast capacity to "draw back" and constrict thoughts, feelings, and sensations, as well as an equivalent capacity to "burst forth" and expand thoughts, feelings, and sensations. At the same time, each of these capacities is delimited. We can only constrict (e.g., focus, accommodate) and expand (e.g., enlarge, assimilate) so far before the givens of existence—such as death, genes, and culture—deter and curtail us. For Schneider, it is the interplay among constrictive and expansive capacities, the ability to respond to those capacities, and the ability to integrate those responses into a dynamic whole that constitute personal and interpersonal richness and health.

In more recent years, Schneider (1995, 2008) has developed an "existential–integrative" (EI) approach to therapy. This approach holds that levels of "liberation," such as the physiological, the environmental, and the interpersonal, are interwoven into the constrictive/expansive continuum. EI therapy is now at the vanguard of a broadened and steadily growing E–H practice philosophy (Bradford, 2007; Wampold, 2008; Watson & Bohart, 2001). This practice philosophy draws from conventional E–H principles but differs in one major respect—scope of practice. While the conventional E–H model emphasizes only the experiential level of client contact and thus restricts its practice base, the EI model explicitly embraces diverse levels of client contact and thus expands its capacity to serve. Put another way, the EI approach arose out of the need to address today's ethnically and diagnostically diverse clinical populations, whereas the older E–H modality arose out of a narrower set of priorities (May, 1958a; Schneider, 2008). Within that context, EI interventions are viewed as "liberation conditions" and client dysfunctions as "levels of freedom" or choice (Schneider, 2008, p. 35). Liberation conditions can represent a wide range of interventions, ranging from the relatively "nonexperiential" medical and behavioral strategies, to the "semi-experiential" psychoanalytic and intersubjective modalities, to the relatively "experiential" existential and transpersonal approaches. Depending on the client's desire and capacity for therapeutic change, EI therapy proceeds holistically toward an experiential level of contact. By *holistically*, we mean that even when EI therapy is engaged non- or semi-experientially, it is still engaged within an ever-varying, ever-available experiential context.

To sum, as we explore the theory and practice of E–H therapy, we will also elaborate the EI approach, trace its relevance to E–H therapy, and apply it to diverse cases.

Buber, Friedman, and Yalom: The Dialogical or Interpersonal Dimension

Yet another expression of existential practice emphasizes the immediate, "here and now" encounter. Echoing the philosophy of Martin Buber, Maurice Friedman (1995, 2001) has developed a "dialogical" approach to psychological functioning. The dialogical approach, based on Buber's philosophy of "I–Thou" relationships, accents the interpersonal and interdependent dimension of personality. For Friedman, psychological growth and development proceed, not merely or mainly through the encounter with self, but through the encounter with another. This "healing through meeting" as Friedman puts it, is characterized by the ability to be present to and confirming of oneself, while at the same time being open to and confirming of another. The freedom and limits of such a relationship then become transferred to the freedom and limits experienced within one's self and the trust developed to risk affirmation of the self.

Yalom (2002) is another existential therapist who values the "I–Thou" relationship. Yalom believes that change and growth occur *only* within the context of a safe and intimate therapeutic relationship. Clients, who typically have difficulty forming intimate relationships in their lives, learn how to create one with the therapist. It is within the safety of this intimate relationship that clients can face and accept the givens of existence and choose to live differently. Consequently for Yalom, building an intimate therapeutic relationship with his client is the central task because it "will itself become the agent of change" (2002, p. 34).

CLINICAL ASSESSMENT: THE CAPACITY FOR PRESENCE

The question of assessment is essentially the question of understanding: On what basis do E–H therapists understand an individual's pattern of interaction, symptomatology, and adaptive resources? E–H therapists employ a variety of means to understand their clients' lives. Among these means can be paper and pencil tests, ratings of symptomatology, and history taking. However, these modalities tend to be implemented sparingly rather than as a staple of practice. The reason for this caveat is that, as a rule, assessment—like therapy—is an ongoing process for E–H practitioners, and not a linear or mechanistic procedure. Appraisal is holistic, in other words, and should not be mistaken for a global or rigid declaration (Bugental & Sterling, 1995). Client X may be a "depressive" for an E–H practitioner, but he is also a living, dynamic human being, and this is pivotal information both for client and therapist.

E–H practitioners are concerned with depth and breadth of context as much as or more than they are with specific overt behaviors. Ideally, nothing is spared in E–H therapeutic assessment: The unfolding moment, the client's explicit and implicit intentions in the moment, the horizons of the past, and the full person-to-person field that is evoked each moment are of equal and abiding import (Fischer, 1994; Schneider, 2008).

As previously indicated, contemporary E–H practice tends to be an integrative practice (Schneider, 2008; Watson & Bohart, 2001). E–H practitioners value the whole human being—conscious and nonconscious, past, present, and evolving—in the therapeutic encounter. As such, E–H practitioners are concerned with how best to understand clients in their moment-to-moment unfolding and their given level of relation and experience.

The client's capacity for intra- and interpersonal presence is the chief tool of E–H assessment. Through presence, the holding and illuminating of clients' moment-to-moment experience, E–H therapists become attuned to the subtlest nuances of clients' concerns, from the cognitive and behavioral to the affective and spiritual.

Although E–H therapists value the content (or explicit features) of clients' experiences, they are acutely and simultaneously attuned to the process or implicit aspects of those experiences. The following example[1] from Orah Krug will serve to illustrate:

> Recently I was sitting with a crying client. As I listened to her story, I noticed that she refused to take another tissue even though the

---

[1] All case material in this volume is disguised. In most instances, case material entails a composite, drawn from our respective practices.

one she was using was torn and tattered. I gently commented at an appropriate time on her refusal to take another tissue. Her eyes welled up with more tears as she realized that this behavior was a familiar way of being, and she said, "I always just make do with what I have."

This attunement to process presupposes that each person is related to self, to other, and to the physical world and also that each person's past is present in the here and now. That is, each person shapes her or his past experiences into a unique sense of self that is in some way evident in the here and now. Using these assumptions as a basis for my work, I focused on the unfolding intra- and interpersonal processes with the intention of understanding this client's underlying subjective constructs of self and world. Self and world constructs refer to the client's construal of existence, both conscious and subconscious, as derived from the client's unique shaping of her or his subjective experiences with the objective world (May's "passion for form"). Thus, one part of my client's shaped sense of self is that she "always just makes do with what she has." Consequently, she relates to herself and to me in that way, and this construct of herself and her world is concretely reflected in her "tissue behavior."

The E–H therapist understands that the underlying nature of a problem may be different than the surface content. For example, whereas the content of a client's report (e.g., binge eating) may be physiological in nature, the process or implicit aspects may be intensely spiritual, ontological, or interpersonal in nature. E–H assessment, therefore, is predicated on not only a client's presenting problem (or complaint), but also the entire atmosphere of a client's predicament. Everything and anything is open to investigation within the E–H framework, from the initial manner in which the client greets the therapist to the position of the client's hands while elaborating her concern. Put another way, every E–H assessment is holographic. Every moment is believed to be a microcosm and in some sense dovetails with every other moment. No moment stands in isolation.

To illustrate further, one of the first areas of focus within E–H therapy—even before any words are exchanged—are questions such as: What is my client expressing in his body and in what ways are those expressions indicative of my client's self and world construct? How does he relate to himself and how does he relate to me? The E–H therapist is particularly attuned to the manner in which these expressions resonate within herself or himself—their shape, texture, and future intimations. In effect, the E–H therapist uses her or his body as a barometer or register of clients' tacit and overt struggles. Here is a sample of our own thoughts upon greeting a given client:

> What is this man's sense of self and world? What kind of life-design do his muscles, gestures, and breathing betray? Is he stiff and waxy or limber and fluid? Is he caved in and hunched over or stout and thrust forward? Does he curl up in a remote corner of the room or does he "plant himself in my face"? What does he bring up in *my* body? Does he make me feel light and buoyant or heavy and stuck? Do my stomach muscles tighten, or do my legs become jumpy? Do my eyes relax, or do they become "hard" or guarded? What can I sense from what he wears? Is he frumpy and inconspicuous or loud and outrageous? What can be gleaned from his face? Is it tense and weather-beaten or soft and innocent? Does he meet my gaze or turn away? (See Schneider, 2008, p. 61, for an elaboration.)

Each of these observations begins to coalesce with others, cumulatively, to disclose a unique world. Each oscillates with others to form a shape, sense, and overarching gestalt of this particular man's strife and life patterns.

Intra- and interpersonal presence then is the sine qua non of E–H assessment. Through the illumination of presence, E–H therapists open to and begin to discover clients' constructs of self and world, overt and covert scripts, ostensible and tacit agendas, and unfolding rivalries within the battleground of self. Further, they begin to sense the shape of their own responses to these revelations and how best to "meet" or facilitate them. For example, an E–H therapist might ask (silently to herself), what are the resources, difficulties, and potential tools necessary to address an acutely fragile client? What about a combative client or a client who resists exploration? These are issues that challenge any serious-minded therapist, but are especially trying to E–H practitioners who prize depth of connection over symptom relief. The question for the E–H therapist is, How can I best meet this client "where he or she lives," within the abilities and constraints of where he or she lives, and yet hold out the possibility for a fuller and deeper connection? This holding out of the possibility for an enlarged and deepened contact is one of the primary distinctions between mainstream and E–H visions of healing. Whereas mainstream practitioners may tend to calibrate their actions to given parts of the therapeutic concern (e.g., those that pertain to behavior or cognition or childhood), E–H practitioners endeavor to be available to clients in their multilayered and emergent wholeness, from the measurable and overt to the felt and unformed. It is in this sense that diagnosis is a part of the ongoing contact in E–H therapy, and that formulations must fit people, and not the other way around (Fischer, 1994; May, 1983).

Given its evolving and holistic approach, then, E–H assessment must be artfully and mindfully engaged. While psychiatric diagnoses may be useful to E–H practitioners at given stages of therapy, the assessment overall is based on therapist attunement, experience, and clinical judgment. As a rule, the client's desire and capacity for change and the therapist's mindful and sensitive alertness to these criteria guide the ensuing work.

4

The Therapy Process

As we established in chapter 3, the aim of existential–humanistic (E–H) therapy is to "set clients free." However when we speak of this, we do not at all mean helping clients to become capricious or licentious louts. What we do mean is helping clients to cultivate the capacity for choice; and choice, as is well established in the existential literature, implies limits, ambiguities, and risks (May, 1981; Tillich, 1952) about which E–H therapists and clients alike become acutely aware. At the same time, choice is cherished as the point of being alive in E–H therapy, in spite of and perhaps even in light of its inherent difficulties.

Given that contemporary E–H therapy is both integrative and incremental in its approach to freedom, the practitioner faces an array of choice points on her or his facilitative journey. The client's desire and capacity for change (Schneider, 2008), the alliance and context of the therapy (Bugental, 1987), and practical elements (Yalom, 1989) all figure in. Hence, for some E–H clients, at some stages of therapy, choice can mean drug-induced stability,

The case of James is from "The Experiential Liberation Strategy of the Existential–Integrative Model of Therapy," by K. Schneider, 2007, *Journal of Contemporary Psychotherapy, 37*, p. 36. Copyright 2007 by Springer. Reprinted with permission of Springer Science and Business Media.

or nutrition-based evenness of mood, or reasoned-based empowerment, for example. However, that which distinguishes E–H facilitation is its ability to address, not merely programmatic (i.e., externally based) adjustments, but internally sparked commitments. Commitment, for E–H therapists, refers to a sense of "I-ness," agency, or profound caring about a given direction (May & Yalom, 1995). It implies assumption of personal responsibility and a sense that the life one chooses really matters to oneself and is worth one's whole (embodied) investment (Bugental, 1987). This ontological or experiential level of commitment manifests clinically as a sense of immediacy (aliveness), affectivity (passion), and kinesthesia (embodiment) and is typified in the deepest and most pivotal stages of therapy. In short, E–H therapists endeavor to meet clients "where they are at," but also to be available to the fullest potential of those clients to "own" or claim the life that is presented to them.

In light of this background, E–H therapy can vary in both length and intensity. It can proceed, on rare occasions, within one or two sessions (e.g., Galvin, 2008; Laing, 1985), or it can occur in a limited way within a short-term focused format (e.g., Bugental, 2008). Typically, however, E–H engagements are intimate (e.g., trust-building), long-term (e.g., 3–5 years), and intensive (e.g., weekly to twice weekly). Furthermore, E–H therapy can be of benefit to a more diverse range of clientele than is generally presumed (e.g., see May, 1972; Vontress & Epp, 2001), although those who tend to be introspective, emotionally tolerant, and exploratory are likely to derive maximal benefits.

To summarize then, the chief question for the E–H therapist is how does one help this person (client) find choice—meaning, clarity, poignancy—in her or his life, in spite of (and sometimes, in light of) all the threats to these possibilities? Clearly, there are no easy answers to this question, yet it is precisely freedom's difficulty, its intensity, that for E–H therapists is key to its unfolding. In other words, E–H therapists challenge clients to grapple with their concerns, not just intellectually, behaviorally, or programmatically, but experientially, to maximize their capacities to transform themselves.

THE ROLE OF THE THERAPIST, CLIENT, AND THEIR RELATIONSHIP

In this section, we will elucidate the major dimensions of E–H therapy as they unfold in action. We will draw on case vignettes to bring theoretical material alive. In keeping with the E–H practice philosophy, therapist, client, and relational roles will be presented here, not as isolable units but as interweaving strands comprising an integral whole. Each role will thus become evident in its interlinking and inextricable context.

Existential Stances or Conditions

To achieve the aims of E–H therapy, practitioners draw on a variety of means. These means, however, are not techniques in the classical sense; they are stances, or conditions, through which experiential liberation and profound transformation can take root. Among the core intertwining and overlapping E–H stances are the following:

- the cultivation of therapeutic presence (presence as ground)
- the cultivation and activation of therapeutic presence through struggle (presence as method and goal)
- the encounter with the resistance to therapeutic struggle
- the coalescence of the meaning, intentionality, and life awakening (awe) that can result from the struggle

Let's consider each of these dimensions in turn.

THE CULTIVATION OF THERAPEUTIC PRESENCE: PRESENCE AS GROUND

Previously, we referred to presence as the sine qua non of E–H practice. There is a very moving story about the travails of the distinguished existential philosopher, Martin Buber, that vividly illustrates the life and death significance of therapeutic presence. As conveyed by Friedman (1991b), Buber was in the throes of a mystical rapture when a curious caller appeared at his door. The caller was a dour and anxious young man who had come to seek Buber's advice: should he (the caller) volunteer to go to the front of a major battle (during World War I), or should he resist and find refuge as a noncombatant? While Buber greeted this young man with his customary graciousness, his usual attunement was wanting. In short, in the midst of his meditative raptures, Buber failed to "meet" this young man, and tragedy followed. Some time later, we are told, the young man enlisted in the army and died precipitously on the front. Although multiple in its potential meanings, Buber took this situation as a dire warning to himself and others to never underestimate the gravity of presence. Subsequently, according to Friedman, he never did.

The gravity of presence is further illustrated by Rollo May's (2007) incisive declaration that in in-depth E–H therapy it is "the client's life that is at stake," and that is how the therapist should view it.

There is a vivid distinction, in our view, between a therapist who approaches a client as a problem-solving "doctor" and a healer who is available for inter- and intrapersonal connection. While the former stands apart from a client to offer a specific set of remedies for an isolated and definable malady, the latter stands with a client to offer a relationship, an invitation, and an accompaniment on a journey. And while the former is likely to appeal to a client's immediate needs for relief, the latter is likely to appeal to a client's underlying urges for connection, self-discovery, and vitality. To be sure, both modalities are often relevant over the course of a given therapy, and both are useful. But in today's market-driven, standardizing atmosphere, rarely are both made available.

Through the dimension of presence, however, (including a willingness to negotiate fees!) both the problem-solving and journey-accompanying modalities can be made available to clients. And clients, in turn, can substantively benefit from these resources. Without the latter (journey-accompanying) mode, however, clients are likely to feel short-changed— and, arguably, like Buber's caller, short-circuited.

Thus, presence is the "soup," the seedbed of substantive E–H work. Yalom (1980) draws an intriguing parallel between the masterful preparation of a meal and E–H therapy. Whereas the average cook prepares a meal in accordance with a standardized menu, the masterful cook, while not ignoring those guidelines, attunes to the evolving, emerging, and subjectively engaging in her preparation. The masterful cook, in other words, has a good sense of how to prepare a basic meal but can also throw in spices, seasonings, and flavorful mixtures that can radically enhance and transform it. For Yalom (1980, p. 3), it is precisely these nonprescriptions, these "throw-ins," as he puts it, that matter most.

Analogously, it is precisely the present and attuned therapist who is prepared to help her or his client most, according to E–H practice philosophy. Such a therapist is optimally prepared to provide the atmosphere, personality, and moment-to-moment adjustments that can mobilize client change (Bugental, 1987). Interestingly, even standardized psychotherapy research upholds this postulate: Wampold (2001), for example, found that "common factors," such as therapist–client alliance and personality variables, account for about nine times the variance in outcomes over specific therapeutic techniques. Yalom (1989) puts it this way:

> The capacity to tolerate uncertainty is a prerequisite for the profession. Though the public may believe that therapists guide patients systematically and sure-handedly through predictable stages of therapy to a foreknown goal, such is rarely the case . . . The powerful temptation to achieve certainty through embracing an ideological school . . . is treacherous: such belief may block the uncertain and spontaneous encounter necessary for effective therapy. (p. 13)

"This encounter," Yalom (1989) concludes, is "the heart of psychotherapy, . . . a caring, deeply human meeting between two people, one (generally, but not always, the patient) more troubled than the other" (p. 13).

Finally, the value of being present as a vulnerable and yet distinctive person, is illustrated by Friedman (1995) in the following client-authored vignette. Following a 4-year therapy with Friedman, his client, "Dawn," reports the following:

> When I think about our therapeutic relationship, it is the *process* that stands out in my memory, not the content.
>
> Up until the time I met Maurice, I had always "picked out" a male authority figure (usually a teacher or psychologist), put him on a

pedestal, and obsessed about him a lot—not usually in a romantic or sexual way, although there was an erotic element. I just wanted him to like me and approve of me and to think I was smart and interesting. A real relationship, though, was terrifying to me—I kept my distance and rarely ever talked to them. The greater the attraction, the greater the fear.

When I first met Maurice, I could feel myself wanting to fall into this same pattern with him. However, I could never quite feel intimidated by him—although I think I really wanted to. He was too human for that. I never felt that I had to be interesting or smart, good, bad, happy, or sad—it just wasn't something I had to be concerned with. If the therapist can be human and fallible, that gives me permission to be human and fallible, too. (p. 313)

For Friedman, as with most E–H therapists, then, the cultivation of presence is the foundation that both holds and illuminates. It holds by supporting, embracing, and opening to clients' travails, and it illuminates by witnessing, disclosing, and engaging with those travails. In short, presence holds and illuminates that which is palpably—immediately, affectively, kinesthetically, and profoundly—relevant within the client and between the client and therapist, and its cultivation is the ground, method, and goal of substantive E–H transformation.

THE CULTIVATION AND ACTIVATION OF PRESENCE: PRESENCE AS A METHOD AND A GOAL

As we have noted, presence not only forms the ground for E–H encounter, it also forms the method of clinical practice and culminates in its goal. To the extent that clients can attune, at the most embodied levels, to their life-limiting patterns of being and to their severest conflicts, healing in the E–H framework is likely to ensue. This healing is a kind of reoccupation of oneself, an immersion in the parts of oneself that one has designed a lifetime to avoid. And it is an integration thereby of the potential or openings that become manifest through that reoccupation.

To help clients recognize their life-limiting patterns and conflicts, the E–H therapist focuses more on process than on content. This axiom is illustrated by the example in chapter 3 of Orah Krug's focus on her client's "tissue behavior." This intervention illustrates how persons in therapy experience their patterns and conflicts as real, in the immediate moment. It also exemplifies how clients come to appreciate the restrictive nature of their patterns and, more importantly, their responsibility in having constructed them. Therapeutic attention to process may vary from an intra- to interpersonal focus depending on the extent to which a particular therapist values an intra- or interpersonal focus (Krug, 2009). Regardless of therapeutic focus, most E–H practitioners assume that the way a person engages in the therapeutic encounter is a reflection of how that person engages in his or her life (Bugental, 1999; Yalom, 2002). Thus, E–H therapists illuminate that which is implicitly and explicitly present at each critical juncture. This experiential method of knowing is an inquiry into the client's and the therapist's lived and immediate experiences based on the phenomenological method (Craig, 1986; Schneider, 2008).

E–H therapists cultivate intra- and interpersonal presence to shine a light on the client's processes or constructs of self and world as they emerge in the therapeutic encounter. For instance, if a client embodies childlike attitudes and behaviors and relates to the therapist as a parent, the therapist would not likely explain this to the client. Instead, the therapist would carefully and respectfully identify aspects of the client's subjective and relational behaviors that are manifesting in the present moment such as, "your voice is so soft and young right now" or "you seem to be asking for my advice"—in effect, holding up a mirror to the client.

The aim is not to explain or interpret but to cultivate the client's abilities to experience kinesthetically and express the ways in which she or he relates to self and to the therapist who is "a substitute for the world" (Trub, as cited in Friedman, 1991, p. 498). This phenomenological approach is an experiential, as distinct from an intellectual, illumination of what it means to be present with self and others. The question for this particular phase of the therapeutic process is: What are the most effective ways and means to activate presence in the client? Or, how can therapists help to mobilize clients' presence (Bugental, 1987)?

Consider the following vignette reported by Kirk Schneider (2007) as an illustration:

My client James is sitting across from me hurriedly reporting on the difficulties he had over the past week. I take a full breath and center myself: "James," I interject, "I wonder if you can take a moment and check in with what you're feeling right now, as you talk about that 'put-down' last week." A little taken aback, James suddenly pauses a moment. He looks inward, and he inhales. "I'm pissed!" he exclaims. "I've had a week—no, a lifetime—of being treated like shit, I turn to a person I thought was a close friend, and even she, apparently, can't stand the sight of me, and I just don't get it—don't know where to turn." [Now James is connecting with himself; he's slowed down enough to be authentically present to his anger, here and now. His life is not just a string of complaints; it has some passion, aliveness, and I decide to highlight that passion and aliveness.]

KS: Boy, you have a lot of energy all of a sudden, James.

James: Yeah, I do—but what the hell good is it? I can get mad from now until doomsday, and it won't change the fact that women think I'm a pervert, men think I'm a weakling, and my boss thinks I'm incompetent!

KS: And what do you think of you? What do you feel toward you?

James: I feel like a jerk—what do you think!?

KS: I don't know, James, I can't speak for you, but I hear you.

(James slouches in his chair as if to fold up in total resignation.)

KS: Where are you now, James?

James [eyes moistening]: I'm stuck, I'm screwed . . .

KS: Looks like some emotion is welling up.

James: Yeah, sometimes I feel like my life is a big wall—and I'm the bug that constantly gets squashed.

KS: Is that where you are now?

James: Not exactly.

KS: Take a moment and be with where you are James.

James: I'm hurting.

KS: Can you describe where in your body you feel that hurt, James?

James: Yeah, it's in my chest—it's all clogged up.

KS: See if you can stay with that feeling in your chest, what other feelings, sensations, or images come up for you as you stay with that feeling?

Summary: This vignette illustrates how invoking the actual has helped James move from a distant "reporter" to an embodied participant. Gradually, as James experiences more and more of himself—e.g., his affect and body sensations—more and more of himself can be accessed and expressed. (p. 36)

As we shall elaborate momentarily, the cultivation and activation of client presence within E–H therapy is characterized by two basic modes or access points—the intrapersonal and the interpersonal. Although it has long been recognized that these modalities overlap and indeed intertwine (Merleau-Ponty, 1962), they nevertheless reflect two traditional E–H practice styles that are gradually—and for many, refreshingly—beginning to merge (Krug, 2009; Portnoy, 2008).

The Cultivation and Activation of Intrapersonal Presence

Bugental (1987) is representative of the intrapersonal tradition in E–H therapy, although this characterization is far from discrete and much about his approach can be considered interpersonal as well. Within the former tradition, however, Bugental (1987) outlines four basic practice strategies, or that which he terms "octaves" for activating clients' presence. These are listening, guiding, instructing, and requiring.

The first octave, listening, draws clients out, encourages them to keep talking so as to obtain their story without "contamination" by the therapist. Examples of listening include "getting the details" of clients' experiences, "listening to emotional catharsis, learning [clients' views of their] own life or ... projected objectives" (Bugental, 1987, p. 71). The second octave, guiding, gives direction and support to clients' speech, keeps it on track, and brings out other aspects. Examples of guiding include exploration of clients' "understanding of a situation, relation, or problem; developing readiness to learn new aspects or get feedback" (p. 71).

The third octave is instructing. Instructing transmits "information or directions having rational and/or objective support." Examples include "assignments, advising, coaching, describing a scenario of changed living," or reframing (p. 71). Finally, the fourth octave is requiring, which brings a "therapist's personal and emotional resources to bear" to cause clients to change in some way. Examples of requiring include "subjective feedback, praising, punishing [e.g., admonishing], rewarding," and "strong selling of [a] therapist's views" (p. 71).

Listening and guiding comprise the lion's share of E–H activation of presence. Whereas instructing and requiring can certainly be useful from the E–H point of view, they are implemented in highly selective circumstances. For example, instructing may be very helpful to clients at early stages of therapy; those who have fragile emotional constitutions, such as victims of chronic abuse; or clients from authority-dependent cultures. Requiring, similarly, may be useful in these situations but also in the case of therapeutic impasses or entrenched client patterns, as we shall see. For the majority of E–H practice situations, however, listening and guiding are pivotal to the deepening, expanding, and consolidating of substantive client transformation.

May (1981) illustrates the value of listening with his notion of the pause. "It is in the pause," he writes,

> that people learn to listen to silence. We can hear the infinite number of sounds that we normally never hear at all—the unending hum and buzz of insects in a quiet summer field, a breeze blowing lightly through the golden hay ... And suddenly we realize that this is *something*—the world of "silence" is populated by a myriad of creatures and a myriad of sounds. (p. 165)

The client, similarly, is almost invariably enlivened in the pause. As Bugental (1987, p. 70) suggests, it is in the therapist's silence at given junctures that abiding change can take root.

The provision of a working "space," a therapeutic pause, not only helps the therapist to understand, but most importantly, assists the client to vivify (or intensively elucidate) herself or himself. This point is illustrated at several junctures in the previous vignette of James but most certainly when Dr. Schneider invited James to "check in with what you're feeling right now." This invitation to pause allowed James to slow down and elucidate himself. As intimated earlier, vivification of a client's world is one of the cardinal tasks of E–H therapy. To the extent that clients can "see" close up the worlds in which they've lived, the obstacles they've created, and the strengths or resources they possess to overcome those obstacles, they can proceed to a foundational healing. Listening elucidates one of the most crucial realizations of that vivification—the contours of a client's battle.

The client's battle—and virtually every client has one—becomes evident at the earliest stages of therapy. For some this battle takes the form of an interpersonal conflict, for others an intrapsychic split. To cite just a few examples, it may encompass the compulsion for and rejection of binge eating, a conflict with one's boss, or a struggle between squelched vocational potential and evolving aspirations. Regardless of the content of clients' battles, however, their form can be understood in terms of two basic valences—the part of themselves that endeavors to emerge and the part of themselves that endeavors to resist, oppose, or block themselves from emerging (Schneider, 1998b). One can understand from this description of resistance and defenses that existential therapy is, as Yalom (1980) suggests, a kind of dynamic therapy that models its understanding of "forces in conflict" on Freud's dynamic model of mental functioning. Again by referring to the James vignette, we can illustrate this point. James's battle appears to be an interpersonal conflict. Although James's underlying relational issues are not revealed in this short vignette, we can see the outlines of it as James expresses his anger at the way he is thought of and treated by people in his life.

Whereas therapeutic listening acquaints and sometimes immerses clients in their battle, therapeutic guiding intensifies that contact. Therapeutic guiding can be further illustrated by encouragements to clients to personalize their dialogue—for instance to give concrete examples of their difficulties, to speak in the first person, and to "own" or take responsibility for their remarks about others. Guiding is also illustrated by invitations to expand or embellish on given topics, such as in the suggestion "Can you say more?" or "How does it feel to make that statement?" or "What really matters about what you're saying?" Finally, guiding is exemplified by the notation of content/process discrepancies, such as "you smile as you vent your anger at him" or "notice how shallow your breathing is right now" (Bugental, 1987; Schneider, 2008). Again referring to the James vignette, we can see guiding in action as Dr. Schneider pointedly directs James to put himself in the equation with these people by asking "what do you think of you?" James's answer that he feels "like a jerk" and his previous lament that "I just don't get it" are indications that James is beginning to face his part in his relational difficulties. Dr. Schneider guides James further to get beyond his fury at constantly getting squashed by others to an acknowledgment of the hurt that underlies it. In this way, James is assisted to experience the complexity of his reactions, beyond his rigidified patterns.

Schneider (1998b, 2008) has formulated a mode of guiding called guided or embodied meditation. This approach has proven pivotal for many clients, particularly those who battle over-intellectualization.[1] Embodied meditation begins with a simple grounding exercise, such as breathing awareness or progressive relaxation (usually assisted by the closing of the eyes). From there, it proceeds to an invitation to the client to become aware of his or her body. The therapist may then ask what, if any, tension areas are evident in the client's body. If the client identifies such an area, which often occurs, the therapist asks the client to describe, as richly and fully as possible, where the tension area is and what it feels like. Following this and assuming the client is able to proceed with the immersion, he

---

[1] Although several variations of embodied mediation have been shown to be highly effective with certain populations (e.g., see Gendlin, 1996; Leijssen, 2006), in the wrong hands they also can be debilitating. As with all approaches discussed in this volume, care must be taken to ensure that facilitation is preceded by appropriate training, skill development, and sensitivity to clients' needs.

or she is invited to place his or her hand on the affected area. (This somatic element can often be, although not necessarily, experientially critical). Next, the client is encouraged to experientially associate to this contact. Prompts such as "What, if any, feelings, sensations, or images emerge as you make contact with this area?" can be of notable therapeutic value. Dr. Schneider reports having seen clients open emotional floodgates through this work, but he has also seen clients who feel overpowered by it. It is of utmost importance for the therapist to be acutely attuned while practicing this and other awareness-intensive modes. Dr. Schneider illustrates this technique in the James vignette when he asks his client to locate the hurt in his body and then focus on the hurt in the chest and see what feelings and associations emerge.

Guidance is also illustrated by a variety of experimental formats that can be offered in E–H therapy. These experiments, including role-play, rehearsal, visualization, and experiential enactment (e.g., pillow-hitting, kinesthetic exercises), serve to liven emergent material and vivify or deepen the understanding of that material (Mahrer, 1996; Schneider, 2008; Serlin, 1996). The phrase "Truth exists only as it is produced in action" (Kierkegaard cited in May, 1958, p. 12) has much cachet in this context. When clients can enact (as appropriate) their anxieties, engage their aspirations, and simulate their encounters, they bring their battles into the room—in "living color"—for close and personal inspection.

While experimentation within the therapeutic setting is invaluable, experimentation outside the setting can be of equivalent or even superior benefit. After all, it is the life outside of therapy that counts most for clients, and it is in the service of this life that therapy proceeds. Experimentation outside of therapy, then, has two basic aims: (1) it reinforces intratherapy work, and (2) it implements that work in the most relevant setting possible—the lived experience. Accordingly, E–H therapists encourage clients to practice being aware and present in their outside lives. They may gently challenge clients to reflect on or write about problematic events, or they may propose an activity or therapeutic commitment (e.g., AA or assigned readings). They may also challenge clients to do without a given activity or pattern. For example, Yalom (1980) challenged his promiscuous client Bruce to try living without a sexual partner for an extended period. This was a highly demanding exercise for Bruce, whose sexual compulsions were formidable and afforded no pause. Yet after the exercise, Bruce reported rich therapeutic realizations, like the degree to which he felt empty in his life and the blind and compulsive measures he took to fill that emptiness. Emptiness, Yalom (1980) reported, subsequently became the next productive focus.

Prompts to clients to "slow down" or "stay with" charged or disturbing experience can also facilitate intensified self-awareness. We have known many a supervisee (and even seasoned colleague) who has had difficulties with this facilitation. They are superb at helping clients to reconnect with the parts of themselves they have shunted away, and they inspire deep somatic immersion in expressiveness, but they are left with one gaping question: "What do I do after the client is immersed?" The exasperation in this puzzlement is understandable. E–H work can seem tormenting. It can instigate profound moments of unalloyed pain. The last thing a therapist wishes to do in such a situation is to enable increased suffering or to hover in continued despair. And yet, given the client's desire and capacity for change, these are precisely the allowances that E–H therapists must provide, precisely the groundworks they must pursue. They must develop trust and a sense that the work will unfold (Welwood, 2001). Hence, what do we advise our supervisees and colleagues? We suggest that it is in their interest to trust—in particular, to trust that gentle prompts to "stay with" or "allow" intensive material will almost invariably lead to changes in that material. While these changes may not feel immediately welcome or gratifying—indeed, they may even feel regressive for a time—they do represent evolution, the "more" that every person is capable of experiencing.

Working with dreams is another venue in which self-awareness and the "more" is cultivated. Dreams represent a restatement of the client's central concern in a language of visual imagery (Yalom, 2002). They are concrete representations of a person's attitudes, experiences, and feelings—a falling down house, crossing a bridge, descending into a basement. Yalom (2002) takes a pragmatic approach to dreamwork, using it to accelerate therapy. Dr. Krug finds it helpful to bring dreams into the here and now by having clients retell their dreams in the present tense. It is also helpful to listen for statements that clients make about themselves and others in the dream as well as the context of the dream. Asking "What is the most prominent feeling in the dream?" and "What is most striking to you about the dream?" can further the process of self-exploration and the "more."

Much of the therapist's task within E–H therapy is to facilitate this "more." In time, and as clients become aware of their wounds, they also tend to feel less daunted by those wounds, less imprisoned; they begin to realize, in other words, that they are more than their wounds, and through this process, that they are more than their "disorder." For example, David felt sure that he was despicable, plague-like, and demonic. His parents had convinced him so over a period of 18 years—not through the usual route of abuse and punishment but exactly the opposite, through indulgence. David was led to believe he was a king, a seer, and a god. He was given "everything" and praised for virtually every routine move. The result: As soon as David hit adulthood, the trials and pressures of college, dating, and vocation, his bubble burst. No longer could he live under his former illusions, but now had to face his incompetencies, inabilities to compete, and his far-from-developed will. The convergence of these factors sent David into a tailspin. His view of himself completely reversed: Now in his 30s, he repudiated himself whereas he had earlier glorified himself; where he once saw a titan for whom every whim was fulfilled, he now saw an outcast for whom every desire was unreachable.

The work with David is highly illustrative of the trust dimension in the cultivation and activation of presence. Although his self-hatred was formidable, it was not irrevocable. The therapist spent many sessions tangling with David's anguish, self-pity, and searing guilt. There were many times when he could go only so far with these feelings and had to warp back into the semblance of self and self-image that he had constructed as a defense. But there were times, increasingly productive times, when he could glimpse a counterpart. For example, in the midst of his self-devaluing, he might suddenly become frustrated and realize moments of self-affirmation—that is, times where he actually liked himself, and liked being alive, regardless of the strokes he would receive from doting associates. At first this realization was fleeting, but eventually, as he stayed with it, it became the major counterpoint to his despairing self-reproach. Back and forth he would swing, between burning self-debasement and gleaming self-validation, including compassion, appreciation, and even exultation at being alive. This latter quality was also connected to his growing sense of outrage, not only at his outdated sense of self, but at his upbringing and his well-intentioned but clueless parents. He began to realize that his lowliness was far from an inherent defect but a product of environment, circumstance, and in part, choice.

To summarize, despite David's repeated resistance and readiness to give up, the therapist's empathic invitations to "give his hurt a few moments" or to "see what unfolds" were crucial to his re-engagement with his larger self. And through this re-engagement, he began to discover that he was so much vaster than his stuck sense of unworthiness; he began to see that he was sensitive, alive, and resiliently mortal—and that these were enough.

The Interpersonal Cultivation and Activation of Presence

The cultivation and activation of presence can also occur through the interpersonal route, or that which E–H therapists term the *encounter* (Phillips, 1980). The encounter is illustrated by E–H therapists in myriad and diverse forms. For example, the calling of attention to disturbances or undercurrents in the immediate relationship exemplifies the E–H concern with encounter, as does the recognition of transference and countertransference projections, as does the encouragement to explore the status of the therapeutic bond at given junctures. The E–H encounter assumes that each person brings her or his way of being and relating to self and other into the therapy room. As a whole, the E–H encounter is characterized by the following three criteria: (a) the real or present relationship between therapist and client (which can include projections from the past but chiefly as they are experienced now rather than in the remoteness of reminiscences, as in the difference between reporting about and "living" transferential material); (b) the future and what is potential in the relationship (versus strictly the past and what has already been scripted); and (c) the enactment or experiencing, to the degree possible, of relational material.

Attention to the encounter or interpersonal is a vital part of E–H facilitation (Krug, 2009; Portnoy, 2008). Buber (1970), Friedman (1995, 2001), Sullivan (1953), and Yalom (1980) have all emphasized the interpersonal—or as some psychoanalysts (e.g., Stolorow, Brandchaft, & Atwood, 1987) have recently called it, the "intersubjective." The reason for this emphasis on the interpersonal is that such contact has a uniquely intensive quality that both accentuates and mobilizes clients' presence. Moreover, a focus on the interpersonal develops the therapeutic relationship by enriching the "in-betweenness" of the therapist and client (Yalom, 1998). An interpersonal focus accentuates presence by awakening it to what is real, immediate, and directly relational, and it mobilizes presence by demanding of it a response, engagement, and address. There is something profoundly naked about the turn to an immediate interaction. It takes the parties out of their inward routine (assuming that is there) and focuses the spotlight on a new and utterly alternative reality—themselves. In short, there is something undeniably "living" about face-to-face interactions. They peel away the layers of pretense and expose the inflamed truth of embattled humanity. There are no easy exits from such interactions, and there are fewer "patch-up jobs" as a result.

Take the case of Elva. A thorny and self-aggrandizing widow, Elva spared few with her humor-laced vitriol. Yet Elva's battle was the profound sense of helplessness that underlay her bravado. Since the death of her husband, and despite her bouts with loneliness, Elva had been making a comeback through therapy. She was just beginning to reclaim her self-worth, and her jokes were becoming less caustic, when the bubble burst and she was mugged. The period following this attack, a purse-snatching, was a trying one for Elva. She was retraumatized, and even her attempts at false bravado fell short.

Yet Elva's battle was clear—she was face-to-face with her worst fears of helplessness, and her wounds were exposed raw. It was at this critical juncture that Elva's therapist and author of this case, Yalom (1989), took a risk. Instead of encouraging her to report *about* her terrors, which might have alleviated some of her internal pressure but not genuinely confronted her wound, he invited her to experience her terrors directly with him. But instead of making it a one-sided exercise, he encouraged her disclosure with some disclosures of his own: "When you say you thought [the purse-snatching] would never happen to you," Yalom (1989, p. 150) confided to Elva, "I know just what you mean." He elaborated: "It's so hard for me, too, to accept that all these afflictions—aging, loss, death—are going to happen to me, too" (p. 150).

He went on: "You must feel that if Albert [her deceased husband] were alive, this would never have happened to you. . . . So the robbery brings home the fact that he's really gone" (p. 150). "Elva was really crying now," Yalom (1989) continued, "and her stubby frame heaved with sobs for several minutes. She had never done that before with me. I sat there and wondered, 'Now what do I do?'" (p. 150). But he sensed "instinctually," just what to do. He took one look at her purse—"that same ripped-off, much abused purse," and challenged: "Bad luck is one thing, but aren't you asking for it carrying around something that large" (p. 150)?

This sardonic quip, which was also an offering to dialogue, set off a whole new direction for Elva and Yalom. "I need everything in that purse," Elva protested. "You've got to be joking," retorted Yalom, "let's see" (p. 150).

With that cue, not only did Elva proceed to open up her purse to Yalom, they shared intimately in the discussion of its contents. Finally, "when the great bag had . . . yielded all," Yalom elaborated, "Elva and I stared in wonderment at the contents. . . . We were sorry the bag was empty and that the emptying was over" (p. 150). But what struck Yalom most of all was how "transforming" that engagement had been, for Elva, in his view, had "moved from a position of forsakenness to one of trust" (p. 150). That was "the best hour of therapy I ever gave" (p. 150), Yalom concluded.

Through sharing that bag, Elva accessed more vulnerability, more anxieties about trust, and more possibilities for risking, healing, and bridging than she would likely ever have, had she simply reflected on its contents. By inviting Elva to share the bag's contents, Yalom provided Elva with an opportunity to experience an exceedingly intimate moment with him. Yalom (2002) asserts that "therapists must convey to the patient that their paramount task is to build a relationship together that will itself become the agent of change" (p. 34). Yalom's work with Elva vividly illustrates how he built a safe and intimate therapeutic relationship with her.

The interpersonal encounter for E–H therapists is rife with responsibility, the ability to respond to the injured other (i.e., client) such that she or he can respond to and reconnect with the parts of herself or himself that have been damaged. According to Buber, and following him, Friedman (2001), such responsibility entails

> hearing the unreduced claim of each hour in all its crudeness and disharmony and answering it out of the depths of one's being . . . [It entails] the great character who can awaken responsibility in others . . . [and] who acts from the whole of his or her substance and reacts in accordance with the uniqueness of every situation. (1970, p. 343)

Mutual confirmation, or what Buber calls an "I–Thou" relationship, "a relationship of openness, presence, directness, and immediacy," is essential to the therapist's responsibility according to Friedman (2001, p. 344). While there is a place for modulating this confirmation, and no professional relationship can be mutual in the sense of a friendship, such a notion is nevertheless a bellwether, a palpable and reliable indicator, of intensive therapeutic transformation. Why is this so? Because the further that one can be present to and work out differences with another, the more one can generally engage in the same relational dynamics toward oneself.

In her discussion of Sylvia, Molly Sterling (2001) articulates both sides of the responsibility question, and she does so poignantly and incisively. "My client leaned forward," Sterling (2001) begins her case illustration, "eyes intently on me, voice passionately intense, and said to me, 'I just want to be in your kitchen while you cook.'" Sterling goes on,

> Inwardly, I froze. Not one therapist sinew, not one trained muscle of years of practice, flexed into action. Nowhere in me was there a standard response, and I parody our standard psychotherapeutic repertoire a bit here: "Tell me how that would be" or "You would like to be closer to me" or "Our meetings aren't enough for you" or just a genuinely open and quiet waiting for my client to continue.
>
> Instead I reacted viscerally.
>
> In my frozen moment, I saw the dishes left as I hurried out early that morning. I felt my pleasure in my own rhythm of my pottering

about. I wondered how my family would take to this new person slipped into their lives. These images supplanted my unawareness that I could not sustain my client's intense pressure. I felt, in short, inadequate to her proposition. (p. 349)

Sterling took Sylvia's request as a "concrete proposition to which [Sterling] was called to give a concrete answer . . . And so, the gist of [Sterling's] reply carried all of these feelings and many more to which [she] was then blind: 'Oh, you might not like me so much if you were around me more'" . . . And "in one blind stroke," Sterling conceded, "I had cleaved open a chasm of distance, betrayal, shame, fury, and misconstrual" (p. 349).

Caught up in her own discomfiting anxieties about being wanted, needed, and accompanied, Sterling reacted—as would many therapists in similar situations—with modified, low-grade panic.

But, and this is where the existential, I–Thou notion of encounter become so relevant, Sterling did not desist at the point of her anxiety. She did not "fold up" and revert to some stilted or rehearsed professionalism; nor did she abandon Sylvia, either physically or emotionally. To the contrary, she stayed profoundly with her evolving distress, immersed in it, took time to study it, explored it with Sylvia, and gradually, charily, fashioned a response to it (Sterling, 2001).

The response that Sterling fashioned recognized both her own and Sylvia's shortcomings, but also their humanity. Sterling *was* overwhelmed by Sylvia's neediness in her request, and she had a right to experience this sensibility; at the same time, Sylvia had a right to expect something more from Sterling, something that acknowledged her plea. Sterling took inspiration from the existential–phenomenological philosopher Levinas:

> The ability to respond is the primary meaning of responsibility. Levinas took this further to show that responsibility also carries the experience of being beholden to the other person . . . Responsibility, for Levinas, meant that simply by the fact of the face of the other person, one is "taken hostage"—before thought, choice, or action . . . It is this level of our human condition, brought into presence by our naked encounter, that Sylvia and I . . . had to reckon with. (p. 351)

Although Sterling "failed" to meet the "obligation" of human encounter, in her very failure, she realized, were the seeds of her success. For, as Sterling put it about her discouraging remark to Sylvia, "Sylvia *was* [nevertheless] in my kitchen with me—conflicts, mess, hurry, and all. At that moment, [Sylvia] had what she would get in my kitchen in actuality, if not what she wanted in feeling. I was as naked as she was, if only she (and I) could see it" (p. 352).

But Sterling did see it. In time, she acknowledged how overwhelmed she was by Sylvia's fantasy. She opened up some about her own weaknesses, fears, and misgivings, and this, as Sterling put it, "altered" their relationship. From that point on, Sylvia was freed to respond as a person to Sterling, because Sterling, in turn, had responded as a person with Sylvia. But by acknowledging her limits with Sylvia, both as person and professional, Sterling helped free Sylvia to respond to something else—her nurture of herself—and the challenge thereby to actualize that relationship.

To summarize, the E–H cultivation of interpersonal presence is a complex, organic, and dynamic process whereby the entire therapeutic context is taken into consideration. Among the salient factors within this context are the client's desire and capacity for engagement, the therapeutic alliance, and practical considerations. The guiding therapeutic question is, To what extent does encounter build the therapeutic relationship and further the cause of engagement with the client's life-limiting patterns. Or, on the other hand, to what extent does encounter do the opposite, and defeat or stifle facilitative processes?

The Encounter With Resistance (Protections)

When the invitation to explore, immerse, and interrelate, is abruptly or repeatedly declined by clients, then the perplexing problem of resistance, or as we are increasingly framing it, "protections," must be considered. Resistance is the blockage to that which is palpably (immediately, affectively, kinesthetically) relevant within the client and between client and therapist. E–H practitioners assume that resistance, or protections, are concrete manifestations of some aspect of a client's self and world construct system. E–H practitioners consequently appreciate resistance behaviors because they identify the ways in which a client views her or his sense of self and the world. Consider the following vignette from Orah Krug's work with Diana as an illustration:

Our session began with Diana describing, with evident pride and satisfaction, how she had accepted a challenging task from her supervisor and had successfully completed it.

OK: You seem very pleased with your accomplishment.

Diana, exclaiming strongly: Following through on a commitment is very important to me.

OK: There's a lot of energy there.

Your statement seems to have a great deal of meaning for you. Can you go inside and explore its meaning a little more? Just let your mind relax and say whatever is there. [I intentionally slowed the process down here because Diana's energy identified aliveness. I try to encourage more of that with a person who typically tamps it down, as is Diana's tendency. I sensed a part of Diana was attempting to emerge, and so I invited her to make "space" for it.]

Diana: It's about being responsible, showing up in life, growing as a person. [Suddenly she stopped, laughed and said:] I don't know where I'm going.

OK: You're doing just fine. [I immediately realized my mistake. My comment was an attempt to rescue her from her discomfort instead of allowing her to explore and understand what had just happened. I backtracked and tried to have her get curious about her process.]

OK: Did you notice that your comment about not knowing where you're going seemed to stop you dead in your tracks? Go inside and see if you can discover what's happening in there.

Diana [smiling]: I thought I was saying something stupid, blah, blah, blah, and I thought you thought so too.

OK: You know in that moment of stopping yourself, you stopped showing up for yourself. The irony is that before you stopped yourself, you were showing up for yourself. Perhaps showing up for yourself triggers some fear?

Diana [quiet for a moment and then with tears in her eyes]: Yes, a fear of being out there and not knowing what's coming—I squish myself.

OK: So when some feeling is emerging inside, you get afraid? Can you go slow and explore what scares you in the emerging?

Diana: I feel exposed, I feel vulnerable.

OK: Can you imagine another feeling you could have instead of fear?

Diana: I could be curious—that's how I was last week, when I went out with a group of friends from work. I realized I was attracted to one of the men in the group and felt that curiosity.

I thought, there are a lot of men out there that I could feel this way with, instead of going to that fear place of there's only one man and I have to attach to him.

OK: How is it to share this with me?

Diana: I feel a little shy, but okay. I didn't realize how and why I stop myself and it feels good to have us both knowing what goes on with me.

Comment from Orah Krug: This crucial therapeutic moment could have been lost if I hadn't recognized that reassuring Diana in her moment of discomfort was not facilitative. Diana needed support to explore her repetitive pattern of stopping herself when feeling "out there and stupid." A more therapeutic response prepared the soil for her to embody her silent, constricted way of being constructed long ago to avoid feelings of vulnerability and exposure. Diana's painful shame-based feelings were so palpable that I reactively tried to protect her from them. My experience emphasizes how quickly subconscious reactivity can take the place of conscious presence. This session marked a turning point in our work. Since Diana and I were now both aware of her shame-based constrictive pattern, our work focused on having the "light of day" shine on her sense of shame and not "okayness." Eventually, she was able to acknowledge, accept, and ultimately dissolve those shameful feelings. As that happened, Diana grew into her womanhood.

This session illuminates what it means to cultivate presence and work with the client's resistance to expansion. It helps us understand "resistance" as a protective mechanism and as an expression of the client's underlying sense of self and world constructs. As is often the case, clients bring these protective, patterned ways of being into the relationship and transfer onto the therapist particular attitudes and beliefs that express their underlying sense of self in relation to the other. E–H therapists' understanding of transference is articulated well by Bugental (1965) as " a patterned way of being in the world that involves a significant other and that is reactivated in the patient's relation to the therapist" (p. 138). In Diana's case she experienced herself as "stupid" and Dr. Krug as the "judgmental other." It is important to work with these negative transferences when they arise and give clients corrective emotional experiences.

There are several caveats that must be borne in mind when considering client resistance. First, therapists can be mistaken about resistance. What therapist A, for example, labels resistance may in fact be a refusal on the part of client B to accept therapist A's agenda for her. Resistance is mostly a safety issue for clients—as in Diana's case—or an issue of cultural or psychological misunderstanding. From an E–H perspective, it is of utmost importance that therapists suspend their attributions of resistance and discern their relevant contexts (see Cooper, 2008).

Second, it is crucial to respect resistance, from an E–H point of view. Resistance is a lifeline to many clients and as miserable as their patterns may be, this lifeline represents the ground or scaffolding of an assured or familiar path. Although this path may seem crude or even suicidal, to clients who experience it, it is starkly preferable to the alternatives (May, 1983). Accordingly, it is important for E–H therapists to tread mindfully when it comes to resistance; acknowledging to clients *both* its life-giving *and* life-taking qualities. Bugental's (1987) conceptualization of resistance as a person's "spacesuit" is useful because it metaphorically describes its essence and purpose—that is, as a pattern of being that is life affirming *and* life limiting.

Finally, it is also important to be cognizant of challenging clients' resistance prematurely, lest such challenges exacerbate rather than alleviate defensive needs. A safe and intimate therapeutic relationship must be in place before challenging clients' protective patterns of being.

From an E–H point of view, resistance work is mirroring work. By mirroring work, we mean the feeding back and elucidation of clients' monumental experiential battle. As suggested earlier, this battle consists of two basic factions: the side of the client that struggles to emerge (e.g., to liberate from, transcend, or enlarge her or his impoverished world) and the side that vies to suppress that emergence and revert. Whereas the activation of presence (e.g., the calling of attention to what is alive) mirrors clients' struggles to emerge, resistance work elucidates clients' barriers to that emergence and the ways and means they immobilize.

Clients' barriers are often outside of their awareness, and as seen in the session with Diana, sometimes clients' barriers are outside therapists' awareness. Consequently the E–H therapist must be deeply attuned to herself or himself, the relationship, and the client in order to effectively illuminate what is actual but unregarded, both interpersonally and intrapsychically. The resistance or protection patterns that unfold in the encounter enable the therapist and client to give direct and immediate attention to them, thereby having immediate impact on the client's life. By holding up a relational mirror, the E–H therapist helps clients experience the ways in which they create their life situations and their problems. This awareness hopefully leads to their assumption of responsibility, which is the first step toward changing their lives. The E–H practitioner understands resistance or protection patterns as multidimensional.

A case example will help illustrate these resistance or protection patterns and show how an E–H therapist (in this case, Orah Krug) understands them as multidimensional. Hank came to therapy wanting to improve his relationships with women. Hank was often late for therapy, checking it off his "to-do" list, and wanting me to just tell him what to do so he can find a "good woman." Hank holds himself up as an object to be analyzed. I recognized that Hank's analytic and passive stance made it difficult for him to take responsibility for the way his life was turning out.

The first evidence of resistance (interview resistance) usually occurs in the first few sessions. When I pointed out Hank's persistent tardiness, for example, Hank deflected my comments with no real interest in exploring his tardy behavior saying, "I often get busy with work and lose track of time. It has nothing to do with therapy, I'm always late." I understood that Hank's lateness is not an isolated event, but a segment of a larger life pattern (life–pattern response). Hank is not ready to accept that his tardiness is a resistance to therapy because it's a familiar way of being.

Helping Hank to see that his tardiness is part of a constellation of patterns that are limiting his functioning and truncating his ability to have the satisfaction and fulfillment that he wants (life-limiting processes) is a crucial step. Soon Hank begins to realize that just 60% of him shows up for therapy, just as in the rest of his life. "If I never fully show up, I don't expose myself to the risk of getting hurt." In his interior life, Hank is dysfunctionally expansive. To distract himself from what he's feeling, he's either fantasizing about being blissfully happy with a woman or plotting revenge on her for scorning him. In the meantime on the outside, he runs from activity to activity, never engaging deeply in his work or in relationships and at the same time wondering, "How did I end up being 40 and alone?"

Another resistance dimension is that of the self and world construct system. This dimension is commensurate with Bugental's "spacesuit" concept. Each of us needs to construct a conception of who we are and what the world is. We all shrink the world to a proportion that feels safe. Hank treats himself like an object and sees people as objects as well. Fearing rejection everywhere, he never risks it and consequently never really commits to anything or anyone. His rationalization is, "I really didn't want it anyway," or "they were really jerks for not appreciating me." He creates an internal fantasy world and externally focuses on one detail after another, rarely stopping to experience his feelings of emptiness and loneliness. If he does, he runs a little faster.

Resistance work with Hank involves helping him experience his life-limiting patterns of behavior, which he created to protect himself from pain but which ultimately limit his ability to commit to anything or anyone.

The impersonal, almost mechanical, way that Hank relates to me suggests than an interpersonal focus would be helpful to teach Hank about empathy. After he had repeatedly been late to therapy, I began our next session by asking, "How do you imagine I feel when you come late to our meetings?" He seemed stunned by my question. He said he never considered that his behavior would affect me. My question marked a turning point in our relationship. From then on we used our relationship as the medium in which to cultivate Hank's empathy for others as well as for himself.

As Hank's layers of resistance or protections peeled away, he has been able to face his unfaceable fear, that he is unlovable. Eventually Hank was able to acknowledge his painful belief of unlovability because he feels accepted and safe in our relationship. Our "healing through meeting" allows Hank to develop more empathy for me and for himself and ever so slowly, to begin to like who he is and to reach out to others. Hank's self and world construct system have enlarged, ironically, to include his soft and vulnerable side, which led him to see himself as an acceptable man in a world populated with accepting people.

There are two basic forms of resistance work: vivification and confrontation. Vivification of resistance is the intensification of clients' awareness of how they block or limit themselves. Specifically, vivification serves three basic functions: (a) it alerts clients to their defensive worlds (i.e., their self and world constructs); (b) it apprises them of the consequences of those worlds; and (c) it reflects back the counterforces (or counterwill, as Rank, 1936, put it) aimed at overcoming those worlds. There are two basic approaches linked to vivifying resistance—noting and tagging. Noting apprises clients of initial experiences of resistance. For example: "You suddenly get quiet when the subject of your brother arises." "You laugh when speaking of your pain." "We were just speaking about your anxieties working with me and you suddenly switched topics." "I sense that you're holding down your anger right now."

In a distinctly dramatic illustration of noting resistance, Bugental (1976) reported a highly stilted initial interview with a client in which decorum rather than genuine feeling permeated. Laurence, Bugental's client, took extensive pains to show how competent he was, how many accolades he had won, and how important his life was. But after some period of this self-puffery, Bugental (p. 16) "took a calculated risk." Instead of placating his new client or emulating the standard intake role of detached observer, Bugental turned to Laurence, faced him directly, and averred, "You're scared shitless." At that, Laurence shed his mask of bravado, and began a genuine interchange with Bugental.

Sometimes noting resistance takes the form of nonverbal feedback. For example, just sitting with clients in their uncertainty at a given moment can feed back to them the realization that a change or mobilization of some sort is necessary in their life. Or through the therapist's mirroring of clients' crossed arms or furrowed brow, clients may begin to become clearer about how closed they have been or how tensely they hold themselves.

Tagging alerts clients to the repetition of their resistance. Consider these examples of tagging: "So here we are again; at that same bitter place." "Every time you note a victory, you go on and beat yourself up." "You repeatedly insist on the culpability of others." "What is it like to feel helpless again?" Like noting, tagging implies a subtle challenge, a subtle invitation to reassess one's stance. Implicitly, it enjoins clients to take responsibility for their self-constructions and to revisit their capacities to transform.

Revisitation is a key therapeutic dimension. Every time clients become aware of how they stop (or deter) themselves from fuller personal and interpersonal access, they learn more about their willingness to approach such situations in the future. Frequently, there are many revisitations required before "stuck" experiences can be accessed; clients must revisit many frustrations and wounds before they are ready to substantively re-approach those conditions. Yet, as entrenched as their miseries may be, each time clients face them, they face remarkable opportunities for change; and each incremental change can become monumental—a momentum shift of life-changing proportions.

Let's take the case of James again. In the following vignette, Kirk Schneider presses James in an area that therapist and client have revisited many times—being chronically identified with his "lowly" position in society. Although I mainly vivify or alert James about his chronic identification, at points I begin to confront or attempt to alarm him. (We will elaborate on confrontation with resistance momentarily.) Here is the sequence of our interaction:

James: Rachel called me the other day. She was the one friend I had some decent contact with—until I went and stuck my foot in my mouth. She asked me to see a movie with her and I made a stupid remark about seeing a porno flick to jazz up our evening together. She then told me abruptly that she was offended by my suggestion, and that further, she was no longer "in the mood" to go out that night. How could I have done that?! How could I have taken a perfectly decent relationship, a relationship I knew wouldn't go anywhere romantically, and push it off the cliff? There's just no way around it, I'm doomed to be a shit.

KS: Is that all you are, James? Is that what your whole life and all you've been through comes down to?

James: Seems so.

KS: Yeah, you seem insistent on that—you've seemed insistent on that for weeks. Is that acceptable to you?

James: No, but there's nothing I can do about it.

KS: What are you willing to do about it?

James: We've been around that bend before.

KS: Yes, we have, James. Are you willing to go around it in the same way you have before?

[James pauses and looks down. It's the first time in this sequence that he's slowed down enough to reassess himself.]

James: Well, I am sick and tired of it.

KS: I hear you. What else is here, James?

James: That maybe I wasn't as much the shit as I made myself out to be—that I always make myself out to be. That I slipped up—I made a stupid comment, am I gonna condemn myself for life?

KS: Stay with it, James, what else is present for you?

James: A hint of pride, fight . . .

KS: Say more.

Comment from Kirk Schneider: In the sequence above, James is able to move from a tiring and familiar self-loathing to a realization of the narrowness of that loathing and the possibility for something more, some kind of pride or "fight" in his life. Those are attributes that we [as E–H therapists] can build on. (Schneider, 2007, p. 38)

This vignette notwithstanding, a note of caution is called for in regard to vivifying and mirroring clients' resistance. There are clients who grow to resent such frequent revisitations to their resistance and feel that they are being "put upon." For example, Dr. Schneider had a client—let's call her "Sue"—who was seemingly impervious to the noting and tagging of her resistance. I would convey back to her the diversions or closed body stances that I experienced with her at given points, and she would either greet me with blank stares or ignore me altogether. After some exhaustion over Sue's lack of inertia and apparent obstinacy, I finally confronted her about her experience with me. Her response was informative to me, as it was vehement: "I don't want to change," she snapped. "I feel like it is *you* who wants me to change, and I'm tired of that. I'm tired of people—all my life—telling me that I should change, or be something different than who I am. I just want to be accepted for me for awhile, no matter how I come across!"

This "tongue-lashing" was an important lesson about the phenomenology of certain clients. Further, it was a valuable lesson in self- and other acceptance and how, despite all our efforts to increase these, our interventions sometimes backfire. For this particular client, self-acceptance meant just letting her "be"—which in this case was obstinate; any questioning (noting or tagging) of this obstinacy felt coercive to her (just like the people throughout her life who insisted that she be other than who she is). It was not until I understood this position from her that I could more artfully work with her—and gradually, organically, enable change to issue from *her*, not some proxy.

Another form of vivifying resistance is tracing out. Tracing out entails encouraging clients to explore the fantasized consequences of their resistance. For example, Dr. Schneider has encouraged obese clients who fear weight loss to review and grapple with the expectations of that weight loss—not just intellectually, but experientially, through dramatizing an anticipated scene; identifying the feelings, body sensations, and images associated with the scene; and encountering the fears, fantasies, and anticipated consequences of following the scene to its ultimate conclusion. Although clients often find such tracing out disconcerting, they also often find it illuminating, as it animates their overinflated fears, unexpected resources, and resolve, in addition to harrowing frailties. The tracing out of capitulating to a behavior or experience is also highly illuminating. Such tracing out, for example, might take the form of foregoing weight loss and the anticipated fears, fantasies, and implications of maintaining the status quo. The question "Where does this (reluctance to lose weight) leave you?" or "How are you willing to respond (to such intransigence)?" can help elaborate these exercises.

When clients' stuckness becomes intractable, but with a potential for substantive change, a confrontation may be in order. Confrontation with resistance is a direct and amplified form of vivification. However, instead of alerting clients to their self-destructive refuges, confrontation alarms them. In lieu of nurturing transformation, confrontation presses for and demands (or "requires," to use wording from Bugental, 1987) such transformation (Schneider, 2008). There are several caveats, however, about confrontation that bear consideration. First, confrontation may risk an argument or power struggle between client and therapist, as opposed to a deepening or facilitative grappling. Second, confrontation risks the surrender of clients' decision-making power to therapists with the resultant withdrawal of that decision-making power from clients' own lives. Third, confrontation risks alienating clients—not merely from an individual therapist, but from therapy as a whole.

As unfortunate as these potentially calamitous outcomes may be, they are not by any means foreordained. Engaged optimally, confrontation requires careful and artful encouragements to clients to change, but also, and equally important, a full appreciation for the consequences of such encouragements. Prior to decisions to confront, therefore, therapists must carefully weigh the stakes, such as their intervention's timeliness, their degree of alliance with clients, and their own personal and professional preparedness.

Bugental (1976) provides a keen illustration of confrontation with his case of Frank. Frank was an obstinate and reproachful young man. He repeatedly scorned life and yet refused to entertain its possibilities for betterment. At one peculiarly frustrating juncture, Frank chastises Bugental: "Whenever you guys want to make a point but can't do it directly, you tell the sucker he's got some unconscious motivation. That way . . ."

> Bugental responds: "Oh shee-it, Frank. You're doing it right now. I answer one question for you and get sandbagged from another direction. You just want to fight about everything that comes along."
>
> Frank: "It's always something I'm doing. Well, if you had to eat as much crap everyday as I do, you'd . . ."
>
> Bugental: "Frank, you'd rather bellyache about life than do something about it."
>
> [Frank's "pouting tone" changes]
>
> Bugental continues: Frank, I don't want all this to get dismissed as just my tiredness or your sad, repetitive life. I am tired, and maybe that makes me bitch at you more. I'll take responsibility for that. But it is also true that somehow you have become so invested in telling your story of how badly life treats you that you do it routinely and with a griping manner that turns people off or makes them angry. You don't like to look at that, but it's so, and I think some part of you knows it. (p. 109)

This vignette illustrates several important points. First, by intensifying his description of Frank's behavior, Bugental stuns or gently shocks Frank into a potentially new view of himself—that of a responsible agent rather than passive victim. By accenting Frank's "investment" in complaining, he tacitly asks Frank to reassess that investment, and his entire stance, in fact, of treating himself as a victim. Second, the vignette illustrates how a therapeutic interaction can reflect a more general reality in a client's day-to-day world. As Bugental's comment makes plain, Frank's "griping" must turn off a lot of people, and, as in the case with Bugental, this reaction can only complicate, if not exacerbate, Frank's intransigent bitterness. Third, and by way of summary, Bugental's remarks challenge Frank to reassess his whole stance, the issues leading up to that stance, and the necessity of maintaining that stance. In effect, Bugental beseeches, "What is the pay-off of staying bitter, and is it worth the price?"

On the other hand, there are notable times, as illustrated by Kirk Schneider's client, Sue, when such imploring (or even gentle inquiring) with clients is futile, if not outright hazardous. At such times, clients may feel sapped, "spent," or defiantly entrenched. Instead of confronting or challenging those states, which may have the unintended effect of threatening and thereby hardening intractable defenses, the best strategy, from the E–H view, may simply be to enable or allow those devitalizing realities (e.g., see Schneider, 1999a). Frequently, for example, we have found that clients' investments in their resistance directly parallel our own investment in their overcoming that resistance. Further, as illustrated earlier, we have found that when E–H therapists pull back some from our own intransigence, clients' too tend to loosen up and pull back. This dynamic makes sense, for what is being asked of clients, in effect, is to leap headlong into the doom that they have designed a lifetime to avoid. However, to the extent that such clients feel that they have room, can take their own pace, and can shift in their own time-tested fashion, they are often more pliable, flexible, and inclined toward change.

To summarize, resistance work is mirror work and must be artfully engaged. Vivification (noting and tagging) of resistance alerts whereas confrontation alarms clients about their self-constructed plights. Presumptuousness, however, must be minimized in this work. Whereas some clients are amenable to the accentuation and vivification of their life patterns, others are more reticent, and such reticence should not be undervalued. It too can be informative and eventually facilitate a fuller and deeper stance.

In short, the press to "change" is mercurial. The more therapists invest in changing clients, the less they enable clients to struggle with change. By contrast, the more therapists enable clients to clarify how they are willing to live, the more they fuel the impetus (and often frustration) required for lasting change (Schneider, 1998b).

The Coalescence of Meaning, Intentionality, and Awe

As clients face and overcome the blocks to their aliveness, as they begin to choose rather than succumb to the paths that beckon them, they develop a sense of life meaning. This meaning is wrought out of struggle, deep presence to the rivaling sides of oneself, and embodied choice about the aspect of oneself that one intends to live out. The overcoming of resistance, in other words, is preparatory to the unfolding of meaning, and the unfolding of meaning is preparatory to revitalization.

Such revitalization, or what Rollo May (1969) terms "intentionality," is the full-bodied orientation to a given goal or direction. It is different from intellectual or behavioral change because its impetus derives from one's entire being, one's entire sense of import, and one's entire sense of priority (see also the "I am" experience in May, 1983). But intentionality goes beyond singular priorities; it embraces a whole new way to be. Such being draws on the humility and wonder, thrill and anxiety, or in short awe, of the liberation process itself.

By the cultivation of awe, we mean clients' renewed abilities to experience the fullness of their lives—their deepest dreads as well as most dazzling desires—and their rejuvenated capacity for choice. Among some clients, there is also a renewed capacity to experience the mystery, or "unknowing," that envelops all our lives (Spinelli, 1997). This capacity is often experienced as buoyant, poignant, or releasing (Bradford, 2007; Cortright, 1997; Schneider, 2004, 2008).

Returning to Dr. Schneider's work with James, a few excerpts from their final session will serve to illustrate:

James: The grocer gave me a snippy look again today.

KS: So, where did that leave you? Correction, where *does* that leave you?

James: Well, it leaves me in a very different place than it would have a few years ago. Back then, I would've buried myself in shame and self-loathing. Today I moved on. It made me realize how far I've come since those dark days—after that grocer gave me that look, I got pissed, momentarily, but then I took a breath, carried my bags outside, and noticed the air around me. It was crisp and cool. I felt a big refreshing buoyancy inside that reflected the buoyancy and freshness of the day. And then I remembered how much I had going in my life—the budding friendship with Al, the new focus on my computer studies, my relationship with Sonny [James's dog], and the fact that I was alive, OK with the life I've built. So that's how I feel now, it's not all sweetness and light, for sure, but I don't feel so trapped anymore, so driven. And that has afforded me the chance to get on with what really counts in my life—to live it.

Better words for existential and experiential liberation could hardly be chosen, for in the terms of Rollo May (2007), it's not just this or that problem, but one's "life that is at stake"—and this is what therapists, and indeed healers of all stripes must realize. (Schneider, 2007, pp. 38–39)

As the vignette with James illustrates, the coalescence of meaning, intentionality, and awe takes many forms. Sometimes clients find it in on the job site, in the home, with friends, or with community. At other times it takes the form of a sport, a class, or a trip. At still other times, it is without delineated form. The pivotal issue here is attitude. To what extent does a client's life meaning align with his or her inmost aspirations, sensibilities, and values, and how much is the client willing to risk, or take responsibility for, the consequences of those alignments?

The task of the therapist at this stage is to assist clients in their quest to *actualize their life meanings*. This assistance may take the form of a Socratic dialogue about possible ways to change one's lifestyle, or to relate to a partner, or to begin a new project. It may be manifest as an invitation to visualize or role-play new scenarios, inner resources, or concerted actions. It may develop as a reflection on one's dream life and the symbols, patterns, and affects associated with the dream's message. It may take the shape of a challenge to try out newfound capacities in real-life circumstances— a desired encounter, a wished for avocation, a contemplated journey. Following each of these explorations, meaning is further mobilized by encouraging clients to sort through their experiential discoveries. For example, by attuning to the feelings, sensations, and general life impact of risking a new relationship, clients are in an enhanced position to evaluate the significance of that relationship.

Summary of the Primary Change Mechanisms

As previously indicated, the core of E–H change processes is the cultivation of intra- and interpersonal presence. Without presence, there may well be intellectual, behavioral, or physiological change but not necessarily the sense of agency or personal involvement that core change requires. To put it another way, E–H therapy stresses presence to what really matters, both within the self and between the self and the therapist. The cultivation of presence has four basic functions:

1. It reconnects people to their pain (e.g., blocks, fears, anxieties).
2. It promotes an experience of agency and assumption of responsibility.
3. It attunes people to the opportunities to transform or transcend that pain.
4. It builds an intimate and safe therapeutic relationship, which in itself promotes growth and change.

Presence is, at once, the ground (condition or atmosphere), method, and goal for E–H facilitation. As ground, presence holds and illuminates that which is palpably—immediately, affectively, and kinesthetically— relevant within the client and between the client and therapist. Presence in this sense provides the holding environment whereby deeper and more intensified presence can take root. As a method, presence illuminates the client's actual but unrecognized patterns of behavior and attitudes that are manifesting in the here and now. The in-the-moment illumination allows clients to not only experience deep connections with self and others but also to experience how they are blocked from self and others (Krug, 2009). As goal, presence mobilizes clients. It accompanies them during their deepest struggles, their search to redress those struggles, and their day-to-day integration of those struggles (Bugental, 1987; Frankl, 1963; May, 1969).

In addition to facilitating experiential forms of change, presence also guides and provides a container, where appropriate, for more behavioral or programmatic levels of change. The question that presence illuminates is, "What is really going on with this client, and how can I optimize my assistance to her?" Or, to put it another way, "What is this client's desire and capacity for change?" (Schneider, 2008)

Insight in E–H therapy is more like "inner vision," as Bugental (1978) frames the term. Inner vision facilitates an experience of past, present, or future issues rather than an explanation or formulation about them. The end goal of inner vision is not so much to "figure issues out" as to stay with them, attend to their affective and kinesthetic features, and sort out how or whether one is willing to respond to them. To the degree that one can follow this process through, one can become more intentional (that is, concerted, purposeful) in one's life, but also, and paradoxically, more flexible, tolerant, and capable of change.

Interpretations are provided in E–H therapy to facilitate a deepening of experience more than a strengthening of analytical skills. Although a strengthening of analytical skills can certainly be of benefit over the course of an E–H regimen, the thrust of the work is toward empowering clients to find their logical or adaptive paths. In this sense, interpretations tend to take the form of mirroring responses in E–H therapy, reflecting and amplifying clients' rivaling impulses.

E–H change processes comprise both an intra- and interpersonal dimension. The intrapersonal aspect is facilitated through concerted efforts to survey the self, while the interpersonal dimension is facilitated through the naturally evolving "I-Thou" dynamic of relationship. Although E–H practitioners tend to emphasize different aspects of intra- and interpersonal exploration, there is essential unanimity when it comes to the core of these emphases—immediacy and presence.

To summarize, E–H therapy has four essential aims: (a) to help clients to become more present to themselves and others; (b) to help them experience the ways in which they both mobilize and block themselves from fuller presence; (c) to help them take responsibility for the construction of their current lives; and (d) to help them choose or actualize more expanded ways of being in their outside lives. These aims are fulfilled by therapists through their capacity to attune, tolerate struggle, and vivify emergent patterns and by clients through their commitment to, desire for, and capacity for change. Although E–H therapy parallels, and indeed grounds, many other intensive therapies (see chap. 5, this volume), its emphasis on presence, struggle, and whole-bodied responsiveness renders it unique.

BRIEF AND LONG-TERM STRATEGIES AND TECHNIQUES

E–H therapy applies to a diverse session length and client base. Despite its high-brow image, E–H practice has been applied, both long term and short term, to substance abusers, ethnic and racial minorities, gay and lesbian clientele, psychiatric inpatients, and business personnel (O'Hara, 2001; Schneider & May, 1995; Schneider, 2008). Further, a plethora of practice orientations has arrived independently at and adopted E–H principles of presence, I-Thou relationship, and courage (e.g., see Bunting & Hayes, 2008; Stolorow, Brandschaft, & Atwood, 1987). That said, however, the expansion and diversification of E–H therapy is a relatively recent phenomenon; most E–H practice still tends to be long term and take place in white middle- to upper-class neighborhoods with white middle- to upper-class clientele. Yet there is no necessary link between such contexts and successful E–H therapy. As E–H practitioners are discovering, the benefits of presence, I-Thou encounter, and responsibility are cross-cultural as well as cross-disciplinary (Vontress & Epp, 2001).

While E–H therapists realize that they cannot be "all things to all people" and that certain problems (e.g., simple phobias, brain pathology) are best handled by specialists, a definite ecumenism applies to contemporary E–H practice. This ecumenism is correlating with cross-disciplinary openness, adaptations for diverse populations, and sliding fee scales.

Let's consider some examples of brief and long-term strategies (or conditions) whereby substantive E–H transformation was facilitated. We will use this opportunity not only to elaborate our strategies but to animate them in the context of a case.

Short-Term Case: Mimi

The following case is an example of how Orah Krug integrated an existential–humanistic approach with cognitive and behavioral techniques to help Mimi, a young mother, rapidly resolve a recent traumatic experience. Although not central to the therapy, Mimi's Persian heritage, culture, and worldview were also factors in how Dr. Krug worked with her.

Mimi was an attractive, 29-year-old woman of Persian descent, married, with two small children, and 7 months into her third pregnancy. Mimi had come with her parents and sister to the United States when she was 12. After graduating from nursing school, she worked in a pediatric hospital for several years before her children were born. Mimi was referred to me by her primary care physician because she was exhibiting posttraumatic stress symptoms resulting from an incident that involved her and her children. Two months previously, she and her children had been sitting in their living room when a small plane making an emergency landing sheared off a corner of their house. In our first session, Mimi described her confusion; at first thinking it was an earthquake, she grabbed her children and ran to the nearest doorway. Only then did she look around to see the nearby plane and the devastation it caused. As she related the event, I could see how much she was "caught" in the experience; it was as if in the retelling she was reliving the experience. This is a common and unfortunate aspect of posttraumatic stress disorder (PTSD). By emotionally reliving the trauma, she was in effect, retraumatizing herself each time she retold the story.

Mimi seemed to be coping with her fear, horror, and sense of helplessness with an overlay of anger toward the person piloting the plane. "I was just innocently sitting in my home and now because of this person's negligence, my house has been violated, my children were scared, and perhaps my unborn child has been affected. I know I'm not relaxed and happy like I was with my other pregnancies. I'm very irritable, I'm not being the mother I want to be, and we have to live in a cramped apartment until our house is repaired. Mice have gotten into my house and eaten my clothes and shoes. I feel like my things have been defiled," she explained.

The injustice of the event was gnawing at her like the mice that ate her clothes. Mimi was unable to stop replaying the event in her mind and the consequent retraumatization. She also was experiencing a general numbing of emotions, as evidenced in her complaint that she didn't feel the joy or pleasure in life she had known before. Moreover, she expressed a desire to move out of her house now that it held such bad memories. She was very jumpy. Loud noises scared her, and she worried that she would never feel calm again. If all that wasn't enough, Mimi had taken on the responsibility of caring for her terminally ill sister who lived with her parents. Mimi's days were spent at her parents' house caring for her own children as well as her sister and her frail parents. Mimi allowed that she was carrying a heavy load but said she was okay with the situation because it meant that she was fulfilling her role as a dutiful daughter and a caring sister. Mimi explained that in her culture, adult children were expected to care for their elderly parents and siblings when needed. I reflected that on the positive side her tasks seemed to give her life greater purpose and meaning, but on the negative side, they seemed to be not only a physical strain but an added emotional strain to her already emotionally stressed system. By framing the situation in this way, I hoped to acknowledge the value she placed on her caregiving in light of the norms of her culture but at the same time acknowledge its deleterious impact on her. My approach allowed Mimi to feel supported and not judged. Eventually it enabled her to delegate some of the caregiving tasks to a visiting nurse.

Overall, Mimi appeared to have been a high-functioning woman who, prior to the incident, had felt generally happy and content with her marriage and life but whose sense of security was now badly ruptured. Mimi was drained both physically and emotionally, but she was extremely motivated to feel better and get "her old life back." Given that Mimi was set to give birth in a few months, we had a limited time period in which to work. Consequently, I met with Mimi just eight times over 2 months. Her high functionality, cooperative attitude, and motivation contributed to her rapid progress.

My work with Mimi was an integration of behavioral strategies within an existential context. The aims were: (a) to alleviate her PTSD symptoms, (b) to help her be more present to herself, and (c) to constructively incorporate the traumatic experience into her life. I shared my aims with her and explained how I worked in the here and now to help her become more aware of her thoughts and behavior patterns that might be blocking her healing process. I asked her if she felt okay about working with me in this way. She readily agreed, saying that she wanted to do whatever was needed to feel better. I wanted her to understand that our work is a collaborative effort, and so I began with Mimi, as I do with all my clients, to build the therapeutic relationship with my self-disclosures. I don't believe in keeping the process of therapy mysterious. I want my clients to understand the way I work and, more importantly, to have an experience of it in the first session. Throughout the work, I made sure to check in about our interpersonal connection by asking questions like "How was it to share that with me?" or "How has the space felt between us today?" or "What was the most difficult part of our session today?" These types of questions brought Mimi's focus to our relationship. By inviting her to express her feelings about me and our relationship, I intentionally cultivated interpersonal presence and a sense of safety and intimacy between us. I also tried to help her feel safe and understood by cultivating intrapersonal presence. I listened to her "music" as much as her words, mirroring back to her my felt sense of her terror and anger.

After laying this groundwork, I began to focus her on her anger because it was clear that she was stuck in it. She expressed it as a sense of injustice ("it isn't fair, I wasn't prepared"). By tagging these expressions, I helped her become more conscious of how much and in what ways she was expressing this injustice. I held up a mirror to her experience noting, "Once again, you say how unfair it is" or "Can you hear yourself getting angry again as you tell me what happened?" Fairly quickly, she began to agree with my comment that her repetitive statements were gnawing away at her like the mice gnawing on her clothes. I tried to help her move out of her "stuckness" by suggesting that she employ a "Stop" technique (Penzel, 2000). Whenever she heard herself begin the repetitive litany, she was to say, "Stop, I don't need to go down this road" and imagine a place where she felt safe and cozy. I asked her to practice the Stop technique as many times as she needed to in between sessions.

At the next session, she reported that at first she struggled to stop her repetitive thinking but after using the technique for a while, she was able to stop reminding herself of her plight and started to feel better. Given that Mimi was beginning to let go of her anger, it seemed the right time to help her open to whatever other feelings were associated with her trauma. Consequently, I suggested we explore her feelings of unfairness. I shared with her my sense that the energy with which she says "It isn't fair" implies the existence of some important feelings beyond anger. "First take some nice deep breaths," I said, "and when you're ready, turn your attention inward and make some space for your feelings of 'It isn't fair.'" As soon as she began to slow down and breathe deeply, tears began to run down her face. "Are there any words?" I asked softly. "There was no place to go and I thought we were going to die. I didn't know what was happening, and I couldn't protect my children." Mimi was "with" her experience, not "caught" in her experience this time. By connecting with her inner self, she was able to be both in the experience and outside of it. This is exactly what she reported at the end of our session. "I felt different," she said. "I felt separate from them (her feelings) for the first time." Now Mimi could begin to heal. By encouraging Mimi to be more present with herself, she moved from repetitively expressing her anger to experiencing her fear of dying and sense of helplessness in a constructive and healing way.

Over the next few sessions, as Mimi allowed herself to be with her death terror and sense of helplessness, her repetitive angry statements gradually disappeared. Now we could help her dissolve her traumatic memories. I used a modified version of eye movement desensitization and reprocessing (EMDR), as developed by Shapiro (1998), by asking her to call up the memory and view it as if she were on a train and the landscape was moving past her. As she recalled the memory, I told her to tell herself, "This is just a memory. It's in the past. I can let it go by and focus on my safe and cozy place." We practiced this exercise after first doing abdominal breathing for 5 minutes. I suggested that she try to do this exercise four times before our next session. I told her that if at any time she felt "caught" in the experience, she should stop, focus on her breathing, and return to her safe place.

Two weeks went by between sessions. Mimi walked in looking more relaxed and alive. She had found the exercise to be extremely helpful, saying that it allowed her to take a step back from the incident and not feel caught up by it. She reported that she was no longer plagued by the memories and was beginning to feel more alive in her life. She reported that she was sleeping more soundly, was less irritable, and no longer jumped at loud noises. Many therapists would be satisfied with these results and would likely have no further aims other than to consolidate the learning. But as an existential therapist, I sensed that one of the difficulties underlying Mimi's symptoms was her inability to accept a crucial aspect of existence, namely that personal safety and security is an illusion—at any moment it can be shattered.

Short-term therapy requires a therapist to balance time restrictions with the ability to help a person open to her or his self and world constructs that are both protective and life limiting. I sensed that Mimi's difficulties in accepting the accident stemmed in part from an aspect of Mimi's self and world construct system. Mimi held, as most of us do, a belief in her specialness that often results in the unconscious belief that life's contingencies happen to everyone else but us.

Yalom (1980) describes this process quite well: "Once the defense is truly undermined" [as it was in Mimi's case], once the individual really grasps, 'My God, I'm really going to die,' and realizes that life will deal with him or her in the same harsh way as it deals with others, he or she feels lost and, in some odd way, betrayed" (p. 118). This was Mimi's unspoken attitude, and it seemed important to help her explore and hopefully resolve it to some extent within our limited time together.

Consequently in the next couple sessions, in addition to practicing the desensitization technique, we devoted a substantial amount of time working with Mimi's inability to accept the contingencies of existence. As we explored Mimi's feelings about life's uncertainties, she began to realize how she typically coped with uncertainty—by being self-sufficient and by trying to be in control, by being "on top of everything" and "keeping a lid on her feelings." Her phrase "it isn't fair" re-emerged, but now Mimi understood it as her unwillingness to face and accept the harsh contingencies of life. "Go slow," I suggested, "and let yourself explore what it means now." She responded, "It isn't fair that there is no plan, no structure, no protection—anything can happen." After a few sessions of being with her recognition that anything can happen to her and to those she loves, Mimi acknowledged, "I don't like it but I guess that's just how life is." By acknowledging the condition of being unprotected, she paradoxically could now begin to accept the unacceptable. Although she never verbalized her sense of specialness, she implicitly began to accept her vulnerability and finiteness. Because of our limited time together, I decided not to invite a more personal exploration of Mimi's sense of specialness. I felt that given our time constraints, my responsibility was to help her build more effective coping strategies to deal more effectively with an awareness of life's contingencies. Over the next few sessions, Mimi was more able to accept her lost sense of security and build a more realistic view of what it meant to be safe and secure based on her newly formed awareness.

I met with Mimi 3 weeks later and she reported that she was doing much better and that she and her family were returning to their repaired home the following week. She said she liked it even better than before, and she felt better about herself and her life than she ever had. She declared her intention to continue practicing the meditative deep breathing every day, saying it helped her stay calm and energized. I asked her what her experience of our work was together. She said she learned a great deal about who she was and why she did what she did. She reported that she felt more willing and able to face life's challenges even though paradoxically she recognized that bad things can and will happen to her and those she loves.

I followed up with Mimi 4 months later. She and her husband were enjoying their new baby in their rebuilt home. Mimi reported that she felt "like my old self but better." She told me she wasn't taking on as many tasks and finding more enjoyment in her children, family, and life in general. She said she rarely experienced bad memories from the accident, and when they did surface, she did her EMDR exercise. She continues to meditate, feels relaxed during the day, and sleeps as well as can be expected with a new baby.

Appendix A offers a short-term existential–integrative case conducted by Kirk Schneider. Let's turn now to techniques used in long-term therapy.

LONG-TERM STRATEGIES AND TECHNIQUES

We turn now to long-term E–H therapy strategies. In this chapter, we present Kirk Schneider's case of Emma, which illustrates his existential–integrative (EI) approach to therapy. In addition, in Appendix D we present Orah Krug's case of Claudia, which is preceded in Appendix C by Dr. Krug's conceptualization of the phases of change in in a typical long term therapy. Both of these approaches illustrate diverse but related applications of long-term E–H therapy.

Long-Term Case

In this case, Dr. Schneider elaborates a long-term EI therapy, with a particular emphasis on the experiential level of contact. I will use this case to illustrate both the framework within which I understand psychological suffering (polarization) and the means by which core aspects of suffering can be transformed. Although much of this illustration can be understood on the basis of that which has already been described in this volume—particularly regarding constrictive-expansive dynamics, limitation and freedom, and the cultivation and activation of presence—for a more detailed elaboration, see Schneider (2008). See also Appendix B (this volume), "Summary of Experiential Stances of the Existential–Integrative (EI) Model."

Typically, there is a tenuous link between a client's initial presenting behavior and core (constrictive or expansive) dread. Generally, it takes months, even years, to unpack the layers of fears and defenses overlaying a client's core terror and basic defensive stance. This core condition, however, may suggest itself the moment therapy begins. Such was the case with Emma, a dynamic and multifaceted woman.[2]

Emma entered my office on a bright and cloudless day. She was of medium build, approximately 40 years old, and Caucasian.

Emma was also charming. She was vibrant and articulate, and it was clear that she had "been around." She dressed with style, spoke in clear,

---

[2] Parts of this vignette were excerpted from "Existential Processes," by K. Schneider, 1998, in L. Greenberg, J. Watson, & G. Lietaer (Eds.), *Handbook of Experiential Psychotherapy* (pp. 103–120). New York: Guilford Press. Copyright 1988 by Guilford Press. Reprinted with permission.

firm tones, and got right to the point (as she understood it at the time). "There is something terribly wrong with my life," she exclaimed. "I am at the end of my rope."

As I "sat" with this last statement and with Emma herself, I saw a person of solid conventional resources. She knew the societal "game" and how to play it. There was a hardness to her look and her makeup was formed by sharp and careful lines. It was clear that Emma—if she so desired it—had weight in the world.

However, there were signs of strain beneath Emma's tough veneer. There was a fearfulness in her eyes and a melancholy about her face. Her otherwise resonant voice was interrupted by moments of urgency and breathlessness. It became increasingly evident to me that somewhere, deep in the recesses of her world, Emma was in turmoil.

When I invited Emma to elaborate on what was "wrong" in her life, this is what I discovered:

She hailed from a family of four: her mother, father, and slightly younger brother. When Emma was 3, her father deserted the family and never returned. It was at this point that her paternal uncle, roughly the same age as her father, gradually began to replace his brother as "head of the household." Although Emma's mother was devastated by the desertion of her husband, in her weakened state she accepted and even encouraged the uncle's evolving new role. The mother and uncle exchanged some romantic feelings, according to Emma, but this was short lived. Basically theirs was an arrangement of convenience, which everyone in the family grew to recognize.

Although Emma's memories of those early years were vague, by age 4, she knew something was askew. She felt that she experienced something with her uncle that no one else in the family had experienced and that to the degree they did experience it, they suppressed it. According to Emma, the uncle possessed a terrifying demeanor. He was very tall, well over 6 feet, of stocky build, and bullish. Her main memory of him at this early age was that of his booming voice and rancid breath.

Emma's memory clarified significantly as she recalled her late child-hood (e.g., age 9) and early adolescence. Emma conveyed that she had been brutalized by her uncle at these ages. She recalled him literally throwing his weight around with her—bellowing at her, pushing her, shoving her on her bed. She had a clear memory of him forcing a kiss on her and of being enraged when she rebuffed him. Although she did not recall being overtly sexually molested by her uncle, her dreams teemed with this motif and with many other sinister associations.

As I and others have found typical, Emma's reaction to these heinous scenarios was complex. The terms *helpless* or *hopeless* are too facile to describe this reaction. Indeed, virtually all words—much to the consternation of modern psychology—fail to address her layers of response. The closest she could come to describing her earliest feelings was a sense of paralysis. Beyond being an oppressor, her uncle acquired a kind of metaphysical status before Emma, and she, in turn, felt virtually infantile before him.

Yet Emma was no "shrinking violet." By adolescence, she became "wild," as she put it, displaying a completely new character. She became heavily involved in drugs, smoking, and seducing young men. She would leave home for days, periodically skip school, and associate with a variety of "bad boys." Speed and cocaine became her drugs of choice because they made her feel "wicked"—noticed, special, above the crowd. She didn't "take any shit," as she put it, and she occasionally exploded at people, usually males, if they got in her way. She even began raging at her uncle for brief periods, despite his continued dominance of her.

Emma's hyperexpansions, however, were short lived. They were blind, semi-conscious, and reactive. Beneath them all, her world was collapsing— narrowing, spiraling back on itself. The clearest evidence for this was the essential vacuity of Emma's life. She concealed herself behind makeup and laughter. She felt ashamed around peers and classmates. While she was popular for a period, her substantive relationships were a shambles. The men she involved herself with would beat her. She, in turn, would lash back at them but with woefully limited results.

Emma was condemned by her past. As desperately as she endeavored to escape that past, she chronically reentered it. She repeatedly sought out boys and men like her uncle, repeatedly hoped that something—perhaps she or some magic—could transform them from being like her uncle, and repeatedly felt let down by such men and fantasies.

In sum, Emma was traumatized by hyperexpansion. The godlike power of her uncle made Emma feel wormlike. He came to symbolize her world—perpetually alarmed, perpetually confined, perpetually depreciated. Emma found ways—albeit transient and semiconscious—to counter this wormlike position, but her basic and unresolved stance remained wormlike, permeated by dread.

Emma's chief polarization, therefore, clustered around hyperconstriction. Her secondary polarization clustered around hyperexpansion and many gradations in between. In keeping with my EI theoretical stance, I invited Emma to confront her polarized states as they emerged, gradually proceeding to their core.

Following is an illustration of my interaction with Emma at a highly delicate stage of work, after about 8 months of therapy. At this point, Emma had just broken up with a boyfriend with whom she had a fleeting affair, received a disturbing phone call from her uncle, and felt increasingly agitated at work. She had also began superficial cutting behavior on her forearm, which she hadn't engaged in since the beginning of our work. She denied suicidal intent.

KS: Where are you, Emma?

Emma: Pissed.

KS [pausing and taking a full breath]: Yeah, I see that—let it out if you want, Emma.

Emma [glaring, intense]: What do you want me to say? You know the scene. [She shows me the light red marks on her arm].

KS: Yes, I know the scene, but you're living it—that's a lot tougher.

Emma: Yeah, well, I'm not living it very well. My uncle called the other night; all he said was call your brother—he went into detox again. Just hearing his grating voice, his bullying manner, it all came back to me. I broke up with Tim, you know, the *rat*, he wouldn't do shit for me.

KS: Man, you *do* have a lot going on right now—see if you can slow down a moment and stay with what's right here.

[Emma pauses, reflects.]

KS: Where are you now, Emma?

Emma: I'd like to kill him! [She screams about her uncle, tearing, writhing.] Who the fuck does he think he is breaking into my life again, sticking his dirty business in my face again—I don't care if it's about my broken brother. *He* broke my brother! [The floodgates open, and Emma is sobbing furiously.]

KS [delicately, softly]: I'm here, Emma, just allow it—let it out.

[Emma slinks down into her chair. Her weeping subsides, and she begins to free associate.]

Emma: I just get into this hole, like the bottom's dropped out and there's no way to stop. Everything gets dark—everything gets big, except me; I become this little toy doll and I spiral down, down—other figures come in the hole and they brush me aside, they throw me into corners. I'm cornered, stepped on, squashed. My blood is on the floor, but the floor drops out and I keep dropping, endlessly, helplessly. . . . This is how I feel before I cut. Cutting takes me out of the deadness—it makes me feel alive, in control—even for a moment. It's something *I* can do and nobody can fuck with me.

[As I listen to Emma, I become heartsick, but I also realize the significance of this moment. Emma is now directly aligned with her wound. I pause.]

KS: And where are you now, Emma? Do you still feel alive?

Emma: No, that's the tragedy. The aliveness lasts only a few seconds—it always does, whether I cut, snort (coke), or screw somebody. I'm sick of it! Sick of being pitiable!

KS: You suddenly perk up . . .

Emma: Yeah, well it's true. My dark world has been with me too long. It's not all horrific, mind you, it provides a refuge sometimes. I can get away there and form relationships with characters and places that would make most people's heads spin. It's my fantasy land—magical but deadly.

KS: So what do you feel will help you work your way out of that land— is there anything you'd like to try this week that's different?

Emma: Well, I have thought about taking a drive out to my favorite hiking spot. It's been many years since I've been there and I feel a mystical connection with the place. The trees and the animals "speak to me" there—it feels healing.

KS: That sounds good, Emma. Why don't we highlight that as a task for the week? The other piece I must say I have concern about is your cutting. I'm hearing that as much as it gives you a temporary high, it also destroys you in some way, it keeps you stuck and broken—literally, and it does nothing to break your cycle. I'm also afraid that it may kill you.

How about collaborating on a way to stop the cutting this week too?

Emma [mindfully]: Yes, that's something I'd like to do.

Following this pivotal session, Emma's experiential liberation proceeded to unfold over 4 arduous years. We revisited the "dark place" many times and sometimes dropped into it together, but gradually, through ever-fuller immersions, we witnessed Emma's evolving resiliency to these moments, both accommodating to and assimilating their foundational threats. Overall, we experienced the gamut of emotions during our intensive contacts, from searing vulnerability, to panic, to rage, to bottomless grieving, to disappointment with, fury at, and terror of me.

I worked with her to personally and intensively stay present to these feelings and to use role play, rehearsal, journal writing, exploration of our relationship, embodied meditation, dream analysis, and even a 6-month stint of emergency medication, to facilitate this engagement. I also struggled with Emma over her tenacious resistance to (protection from) change. First, I assisted her to explore these familiar yet corrosive stances, then to mobilize her frustration with them, and finally to overthrow and transcend them.

The core of Emma's dysfunction was the dread of standing out. The closer we came to this core, the more Emma fought to deny it. This was understandable; not only did Emma fear standing out before her uncle, she feared the fuller implication of that fear—standing out before life.[3]

---

[3] This realization of the larger fear of the vastness of being alongside of as well as beyond the fear of the interpersonal is one of the distinctive features of the E–H position on suffering; the locus of suffering (as well as health) is not confined to the individual or even interpersonal but extends by association to the "intersituational," or one's ultimate relations to being (see Heidegger, 1962; Schneider, 1999, 2008 for an elaboration).

While the former fear could be explained and discussed, the latter fear exceeded explanations and words; it had to be *experienced*. By tussling with and remaining steadfastly present to this fuller fear, Emma was able to enter a new part of herself. She was able to "hold" that which was formerly unmanageable. As a result, she became more resourceful, trusting, and bold. She was also able to declare herself, not merely before me and her abusers but before life itself. Today, Emma is in a nourishing and committed relationship, is active in her community, and asserts firm boundaries with her uncle. She also has found new resources to realize her avocations: travel, collage making, and hiking. But most importantly, she has found new resources to realize life itself. She still suffers, but she does not equate herself with that suffering. Now when she communes with the woods, it isn't to simply find refuge; it is to linger over and revel in their beauty, immensity, and capacity to renew.

Long-Term Case: Malcolm

Dr. Schneider shares another example of long-term therapy. Malcolm, a 25-year-old African American man, was the middle child in a family of five boys. Malcolm grew up in a tough lower-middle-class neighborhood. Although he had a history of depression, Malcolm had no history of self-destructive or suicidal behavior. Malcolm grew up in a home that centered on his mother and grandmother. Malcolm's father was a traveling salesman and spent many days away from home. He was also separated from Malcolm's mother when Malcolm was 10 years old. Malcolm's mother was intensely religious and belonged to a charismatic church. On many afternoons, Malcolm would find his mother reading the bible or organizing fundraisers for her church.

As a youth, Malcolm was bright and outgoing and centered his time on completing most of his assignments for school and "hanging out" with friends in his neighborhood. Sometimes he got into trouble with those friends and received harsh punishments from his mother, such as being "grounded" in his bedroom for 10 nights in a row and even "head-slapped" on occasion.

In general, Malcolm describes his childhood as one of a "normal kid" who got into "typical" mischief, especially for the neighborhood in which he lived, but who constantly felt put down. These put-downs not only stemmed from Malcolm's mother, for whom he had mixed feelings, but also from the religious philosophy espoused by his mother's church, which he frequented as a child. Being a sinner was "drilled into" Malcolm, and his only recourse, according to his mother and minister, was to repent—to become an obedient "robot," as Malcolm put it. Malcolm grew to despise religion and everything associated with it.

I was aware of an acute struggle being waged within Malcolm. As we sat together, I could not help but feel that there were two Malcolms before me—one who was downcast and exasperated and one who yearned to "break out" from being downcast and exasperated. I was also aware of our racial differences during this initial meeting but did not feel a need to comment on those differences, at least for the time being. However, I did feel a need to acknowledge his sadness and anger, which I encouraged him to express.

Malcolm was essentially lost. He felt like a pawn in the hands of those more powerful, and he had no sense of how to work out of the situation. This self-appraisal was accompanied by a grave sense of having squandered his potential (he had long desired to be a teacher, and occasionally he attempted write poetry). He also longed for a sustained and gratifying relationship.

Although Malcolm and I were constrained to an extent by his 12-session insurance plan, we also decided it was important to stay open to what evolved in our encounters and to renegotiate fees if necessary when the insurance ran out.

The bulk of our sessions focused on helping Malcolm to stay present to the rivaling sides of himself—the side that shriveled and felt like an "untouchable" and the side that seethed and yearned to transform. But we also looked closely at what transpired between us and how this impacted his struggle. Here's a sampling of our encounter at about our fifth session:

KS: How are you, Malcolm?

Malcolm: I'm OK, I just feel beaten down [he lowers his head]. It's as if the fortunes of life have passed me up. I got no job, no girl, and don't have much of a life.

KS [homing in on what I experience as most salient]: What would a "life" be for you, Malcolm? What would it look like?

Malcolm: That's a good question; I haven't really taken that much time to look at that. I think it would have to do with not feeling like a chump so much of the time; like my life would really mean something.

KS: What does it "mean" now?

Malcolm: I've already told you, it doesn't mean shit—I get a job (I don't really even like); I start out decently in the job, and then I'm accused of being too slow [at record-keeping], and then I say something a little agitated because my supervisor is a goon, and I get fired. I go out to clubs to meet a good woman, and I end up with back-stabbers.

KS [we both take a breath]: What's happening now, Malcolm?

Malcolm: I just don't know, I just don't know how my life ended up like this—

KS: What are you feeling in your body right now? Can you describe it?

Malcolm: Yeah it's like a big weight, right here on my chest.

KS: See if you can stay with that a moment . . .

Malcolm: It's no use, life just sucks.

KS: So is that all that you and life come down to, Malcolm? That you're a useless, incompetent, loser?

Malcolm: Maybe so.

KS: Do you really buy into that?

Malcolm: What else should I buy into?

KS: I can't tell you that, Malcolm, but what else are you willing to buy into?

[This question gets in; he takes a moment to reflect.]

Malcolm: Yeah, you got a good point there, Doc; I have been doing a lot of "buying in" that I don't really want to do. And yeah, there are a few more things in my life than just being a fool.

KS: Like?

Malcolm: Like wanting to go on and get a degree in education, wanting to make a difference in a kid's life—continuing with my poetry, which I haven't worked on in over a year now.

KS [taking a chance, pressing a little]: Would you be willing to start on one of those things right here, now, at this moment?

Malcolm: How could I do that?

KS: Well, what if we collaborated on helping you take steps toward looking into a degree program? For example, would you be willing—this week—to obtain and look through one university catalogue describing an educational degree?

Malcolm [after some deliberation]: Well, yes, OK, that's something I could do.

KS: Something you "could" do or something you are willing and wanting to do?

Malcolm: Yes, it's definitely something I'm wanting to do—it's been too long.

In the next session, Malcolm reported with some encouragement that he obtained a brochure from a local school, and was intrigued with the program. He was also hopeful about the prospects for a loan to enroll in the program. Sometimes simple challenges, such as looking through a college catalog, are enough to kick-start a seemingly intransigent life. Sometimes they are not, but they are certainly worth considering and potentially reverberating to in the reassessment of one's life. In our subsequent sessions, Malcolm gradually became more aligned with the "more" of who he is and less patient with a narrow self-identity. The search for, and subsequent enrollment in, an educational program led Malcolm to explore other possibilities in his life. With my encouragement, for example, he started a poetry journal, which also focused on life observations and reflections on his here-and-now struggles. This activity then led to one of the pivotal events of Malcolm's life—his reconsideration of spirituality. As Malcolm revisited the hurts and torments of his religious upbringing, he began to realize that there were moments—for example, in prayer or during spirited hymns—that he felt a kind of love in the air. It was a love unlike anything he had ever felt from his mother (which struck him as highly conditional), and it radiated throughout his whole being, his whole sense of self. For the first time since rejecting religion altogether, he felt as if there might be a force or spirit that accepted him for who he was, regardless of what he did. He viewed this God or spirit not as the punishing overseer he was brought up with, but as the "beyond" that granted and thereby affirmed his existence. (This understanding, interestingly, dovetails with Paul Tillich's notion of accepting the acceptance of God, which I shared with Malcolm. I also shared with Malcolm the following Tillich [1952] quote: Accepting acceptance "is the paradoxical act by which one is accepted by that which infinitely transcends one's individual self" [p. 165].)

We spent many hours exploring this newfound hope, even trust, in the beyond of the universe, as it genuinely altered Malcolm's life. Now, when Malcolm contacted himself experientially, he would often enter into a sense of "at homeness" or a place where he was "at rest." As our relationship strengthened, he was able to find this place even when he felt some discomfort with me, which was decreasingly frequent. We attributed this decrease to the ample attention we paid to what it was like for him to be in relation with me and to observing shifts in that experience, as well as to the flow of his internal experience. Although our racial difference could potentially have been a barrier, it did not seem to be, perhaps because we checked in so often about our general relationship as well as immediate experience. I don't believe race invariably needs to be broached between individuals of different racial backgrounds; the main issue is whether the participants can stay open to each other, regardless of the particular conflict. The reason for this is that it is not two races who encounter each other, but two people, and if race happens to be what is most salient at a given moment (or beckons to be addressed), then that's what should be addressed. If not, then it is a bit of a sham, and may even be more racially insensitive in itself to press the matter (see Vontress, 2001). At the same time, I try to stay mindful of the way that race, or any culturally or politically charged issue, may potentially impact the therapeutic context and to stand ready to address it (see also Rice, 2008). E–H therapy is not simply a two-person predicament; we must also account for the world in which we dwell. The question is how can we account for that world in a way that engenders therapeutic deepening—not to mention relevance and sensitivity—for the client? In Malcolm's case, the issue of race was addressed implicitly through the authenticity of our relationship and our openness to as many issues as possible that impinged on this relationship. Sometimes this readiness to explore is all that is needed in fostering the therapeutic bond; at other times, with a more distrusting client, for example, race or any charged issue must be explicitly addressed.

As the harshness within Malcolm began to recede, he developed a more open and appreciative demeanor. This demeanor impacted his entire world, from his engagement with studies to his relations with friends and potential romantic partners.

In essence, and through many searches of himself, his relationship with me, and his relationship to his past, Malcolm re-formed his relationship to life. Through cultivation of presence, in other words, Malcolm expanded his ability to "see" himself, and this "inner sight," as Bugental (1978, p. 12) termed it, led to key shifts. Moreover, as Malcolm shifted, he edged ever closer to that ultimate shift—his core sense of acceptance.

Acceptance gave Malcolm the sense that no matter what he achieved (or did not achieve), he was alright, that achieving was not the absolute goal, and that the "being" or presence he brought to the achieving made all the difference. After 8 intensive months, Malcolm and I agreed to end our relationship, strong in feeling that he had begun a new life.

OBSTACLES AND PROBLEMS IN USING THE E–H APPROACH

The main obstacle to engaging an E–H approach to therapy is economic. This barrier is evident from the dearth of funding for E–H therapy training programs (Pierson & Sharp, 2001) to the paucity of third-party reimbursements for longer-term, exploratory therapies (Miller, 1996a) to the scarcity of support for E–H therapy outcome research (Walsh & McElwain, 2002).

It is also evident from the struggle of clinical graduate students who tend to be squeezed by debt and harried by short-term, cost-driven training (Elkins, 2007; Miller, 1996b).

Culturally, E–H therapy is also challenged. A core dimension of our industrialized, achievement-oriented society is efficiency (F. Taylor, 1911). Efficiency emphasizes speed, instant results, and appearance and packaging—dimensions that sometimes contrast with comprehensive E–H care (Schneider, 2005). At the same time, the field of psychotherapy is increasingly recognizing the value of in depth, personal dimensions of effective practice (see chap. 5, this volume), and E–H therapy, particularly with its integrative emphasis, is on the forward edge of that recognition. Consider, for example, leading therapy outcome researcher Bruce Wampold's suggestion that "an understanding of the principles of existential therapy is needed by all therapists, as it adds a perspective that might . . . form the basis of all effective treatments" (Wampold, 2008, p. 6).

Further, E–H therapy is being engaged by an increasingly diverse base of practitioners, as evinced by the variety of case studies in the recent textbook *Existential–Integrative Psychotherapy* (Schneider, 2008), along with the growth of E–H therapy training centers, such as the Existential–Humanistic Institute and the Institute for Humanistic Studies, as well as major symposia at the American Psychological Association's Annual Convention (e.g., "Existential-Humanistic Therapy Comes of Age," a forthcoming symposium in August, 2009; see also Pierson & Sharp, 2001). We hope this book, with its call to a more integrative E–H perspective, will be another important step toward both the diversification and expansion of E–H practice principles. Correspondingly, those who value E–H principles need to find more ways to bolster their impact on the profession as a whole. More training programs are needed, even on a pilot basis, along with more dedication to research and more outreach by E–H practitioners to underserved communities. The therapy and theory need to be expanded to concretely clarify their relevance to a diversity of clientele, but also their limitations. There need to be more conferences, debates, dialogues, and collaborations with mainstream therapeutic communities. Bridge building in humanistic books and journals (such as the *Journal of Humanistic Psychology)*—as well as at professional conferences—is a start in this direction, but much more such activity is needed at the levels of academia, research, and public and private institutions. E–H therapy cannot be all things to all people, but it does have a striking potential to revitalize lives. This revitalization can take place across many individual and collective sectors of our society, and this is the next step as far we are concerned, in the evolution of our discipline.

5

Evaluation

RESEARCH SUPPORTING EFFICACY
OF APPROACH

It is one of the supreme ironies of our field that the most salient factors in therapeutic outcome research—a healing environment, the therapeutic relationship, and the therapist's and client's personal styles—echo incisively the precepts emphasized by existential–humanistic (E–H) therapy, one of the field's least studied modalities (Elkins, 2007; Lambert, 1992; Norcross, 1987; Walsh & McElwain, 2002; Wampold, 2001, 2008). As Elkins (2007) pointed out in a recent article, the meta-analytic findings upholding these "context" factors "are a powerful confirmation of what humanistic psychologists have maintained for years" and yet has eluded much systematic inquiry (p. 496). He goes on to note that it's not so much "theories and techniques that heal . . . but the human dimensions of therapy and the 'meetings' that occur between client and therapist as they work together" (p. 496).

Leading therapy researcher Bruce Wampold (2008) is just as adamant. In a review of Kirk Schneider's edited book *Existential–Integrative Psychotherapy*, he writes: "I have no doubt that EI approaches would satisfy any criteria used to label other psychological treatments as scientific" (p. 5). And it bears repeating: "It could be . . . that an understanding of the principles of existential therapy is needed by all therapists, as it adds a perspective that might, as Schneider contends, form the basis of all effective treatments" (p. 6).

Yet as robust as these cited meta-analyses of therapeutic outcome have been, they seem to have had a limited impact on both the training and orientations of mainstream practitioners (Cooper, 2004; Elkins, 2007; Westen, Novotny, & Thompson-Brenner, 2004). The so-called EST or empirically supported treatments movement on the other hand, which established highly stringent—some would say "truncated"—parameters of methodological validation, still dominates the thinking in professional practice and training (APA Task Force on Evidence-Based Practice, 2006; Elliot, 2002; Westen, Novotny, & Thompson-Brenner, 2004). The EST movement accentuates the investigation of overt and quantifiable (e.g., cognitive–behavioral) forms of practice, while neglecting or overlooking the contextual factors (and meta-analytic findings) elucidated previously (see Cain & Seeman, 2002, and Wertz, 2001, for comprehensive reviews).

This state of affairs is shifting (APA Task Force on Evidence-Based Practice, 2006; Norcross, 2002), and existential–humanistic therapy is in a prime position to be a beneficiary of this shift (Schneider, 2008). In the past decade, mainstream conceptions of outcome research have undergone notable reevaluations. Models formerly considered invulnerable are now being revised. The randomized controlled trial, for example, once considered the "gold standard" of (overt and measurable) psychotherapy evaluation research, has been roundly criticized and reassessed (see Bohart, O'Hara, & Leitner, 1998; Goldfried & Wolfe, 1996; Schneider, 2001; Westen, Novotny, & Thompson-Brenner, 2004). Conversely, qualitative research, once considered practically and scientifically untenable, has attained greater professional acceptability (APA Task Force on Evidence-Based Practice, 2006; Wertz, 2001).

In light of these changes, existential psychotherapy has been accumulating a considerable base of empirical support. Although still comparatively small, this literature is both rigorous and promising (Elliott & Greenberg, 2002; Walsh & McElwain, 2002). As previously mentioned, in the domain of systematic quantitative inquiry, there is growing support for key existential principles of practice. This support is worth elaborating. The so-called "context" or "common factors" research discussed previously consistently upholds relationship, as opposed to technique, as the core facilitative agent (Wampold, 2001). This research is reinforced in findings on the therapeutic alliance (Hovarth, 1995), empathy (Bohart & Greenberg, 1997), genuineness and positive regard (Orlinsky, Grawe, & Parks, 1994), and clients' capacity for self-healing (Bohart & Tallman, 1999). It is also mirrored in the burgeoning research on expressed emotion (e.g., Gendlin, 1996; Greenberg, Rice, & Elliott, 1993). Further, in a little known but provocative study of existential therapy with patients diagnosed as schizophrenic and treated at Soteria House, an alternative, minimally medicating psychiatric facility, Mosher (2001) reported the following: At two-year follow-up, the experimental (existentially treated) population "had significantly better outcome" along such dimensions as rehospitalization, psychopathology, independent living, and social/occupational functioning than their conventionally treated counterparts (p. 392). In a follow-up review of the efficacy of all controlled trials (comprising 223 participants) employing the Soteria model, Calton, Ferriter, Huband, and Spandler (2008) concluded:

> the Soteria paradigm yields equal, and in certain specific areas, better results in the treatment of people diagnosed with first- or second-episode schizophrenia spectrum disorders (achieving this with considerably lower use of medication) when compared with conventional, medication-based approaches. Further research is urgently required to evaluate this approach more rigorously because it may offer an alternative treatment for people diagnosed with schizophrenia spectrum disorders. (p. 181)

Another promising area of quantitative support for E–H practice is the neuroscience of emotional regulation. Greenberg (2007), in a recent overview of this area, concluded that for affect regulation to endure, it generally must be mediated through nonverbal (e.g., embodied) therapeutic modalities rather than those that stress cognition. "Cognitive control," he states,

> can be useful for people who feel out of control [but] over time, it is the building up of implicit or automatic emotion regulation capacities that is important for enduring change, especially for personality-disordered clients. . . . The provision of a safe, validating, supportive, and empathic environment is the first level of intervention that helps soothe and regulate automatically generated underregulated distress. (p. 416)

He sums up:

> Looking at emotion regulation in a broader, dynamic systems view, we thus see that much affect regulation occurs implicitly through the right hemispheric processes, and is not verbally mediated. This processing is highly relational, and is most directly affected by processes such as the autonomic generation of self-soothing and self-compassion, and relational communications through facial expression, vocal quality, and eye contact. (p. 415)

Finally, there is a growing body of research in the area of clinical training that also provides quantitative support for existential processes. In a recent review of the literature, Fauth and colleagues (2007) call for a new emphasis on *personal* dimensions of training, including responsiveness and presence:

> Research indicates that traditional psychotherapy training practices do not durably improve the effectiveness of trainees because they overemphasize theory, technical adherence, and didactic learning. Thus we propose that future psychotherapy training focus on a few "big ideas," such as therapeutic responsiveness [and] . . . the development of psychotherapist meta-cognitve skills (i.e., pattern recognition and mindfulness) via experiential practice . . . (p. 389)

On the qualitative side of the equation, existential psychotherapy has produced some of the most eloquent case studies in the professional literature (e.g., Binswanger, 1958; Boss, 1963; Bugental, 1976; May, 1983;

Schneider & May, 1995; Spinelli, 1997; Yalom, 1989). These studies help us to understand lived experience, not just reports about experiences. For example, Boss (1963) has shown how phenomenological dream analysis can illuminate a client's subjective grasp of his suffering; Bugental (1976) has vividly elucidated his personal struggles—thoughts, feelings, and even kinesthetic reactions—in his depictions of his work with clients; Schneider and May (1995) and Schneider (2008) have shown the value of existential principles for some of the least "typical" client populations; and Yalom (1989) has explicated the liveliness and even humor of profound therapeutic rapport.

In the area of more formal qualitative studies, Bohart and Tallman (1999), Rennie (1994), and Watson and Rennie (1994) have demonstrated the value of such existential concepts as presence and the expansion of the capacity for choice in effective facilitation. Successful psychotherapy, they have shown, necessitates a "process of self-reflection" and a consideration of "alternative courses of action and making choices" (Walsh & McElwain, 2002, p. 261). In a related study, Hanna, Giordano, Dupuy, & Puhakka (1995) investigated what they termed "second order" or deep, sweeping change processes in therapy. They found that "transcendence" (moving beyond limitations), which is compatible with existential emphases on liberation, was the essential structure of change. They found, further, that transcendence consisted of "penetrating, pervasive, global and enduringly stable" insights accompanied by "a new perspective on the self, world, or problem" (p. 148). Finally, in a study of clients' perceptions of their existentially oriented therapists, Schneider (1985) reported that although techniques were important to long-term success, the "personal involvement" of the therapist (her or his genuineness, support, and understanding) was by far the most critical factor identified. Such involvement, moreover, inspired clients to become more self-involved and to experience themselves as increasingly capable, responsible, and self-accepting. (See Elliot, 2002; Rennie, 2002; Walsh & McElewain, 2002; and Watson & Bohart, 2001, for a comprehensive review of these and other E–H therapeutic investigations.)

For all its productivity, however, it must be admitted that, taken as a whole, the systematic, corroborative evidence for existential therapy is relatively limited (Walsh & McElwain, 2002; Yalom, 1980). There are two essential reasons for this. First, the existential theoretical outlook has tended to attract philosophically and artistically oriented clinicians more interested in clinical practice and narratives than in laboratory procedures or experimental design (DeCarvalho, 1991). Second, when existential therapists and theorists attempt to conduct research, they find themselves facing an array of theoretical, practical, and political barriers. Among these are the difficulties of translating long-term, exploratory therapeutic processes and outcomes into controlled experimental designs (Schneider, 1998a; Seligman, 1996). It is not easy to quantify complex life issues (Miller, 1996a), and the obstacles to obtaining research funds for "alternative" approaches are, as noted earlier, legion (Miller, 1996b). These obstacles are even more daunting for clinicians who favor qualitative/phenomenological assessments of their work. While such methodologies tend to be more appropriate than quantitative studies to investigate existential psychotherapy's main domain of interest—clients' subjective and intersubjective "worlds"—there are substantial costs associated with their implementation (Wertz, 2001). Not least among these challenges is estrangement from a quantifying/medicalizing research community that tends to deal inefficiently with that which lies outside its purview (Shedler, Mayman, & Manis, 1993).

But this situation, too, may ease as practitioners realize the advantages, both professional and even personal, to practicing from a more intimate, depth-oriented perspective. In a recent article in the *Journal of Social and Clinical Psychology*, researchers found that humanistic and transpersonal psychologists are less likely to experience burnout and more likely to show positive personal growth as a result of their work with human suffering as compared to other types of therapists (e.g., those using cognitive–behavioral therapy; Linley & Joseph, 2007).

Empirical investigation of existential psychotherapy, then, is at a nascent but promising stage. Certain conceptual dimensions related to existential practice have been confirmed by both quantitative and qualitative research, while others await further exploration.[1] If current trends in

---

[1] One of the challenges of this exploration is to tease out the respective degrees of effectiveness among E–H and other, similar approaches, such as client-centered and Gestalt therapies, which also emphasize common factors.

therapy research continue, existential practice may well become a model evidence-based modality that stresses three critical variables: the therapeutic relationship, the therapist's presence or personality, and the active self-healing of clients. From this standpoint, it is conceivable that statistically driven programs and manuals will give up center stage and come to play a supporting role (Bohart & Tallman, 1999; Messer & Wampold, 2002; Westen & Morrison, 2001).

SPECIFIC PROBLEMS AND CLIENT POPULATIONS

As previously intimated, E–H therapy can be effectively applied with a diverse population of clients. Furthermore, E–H principles of presence, I–Thou relationship, and courage have been adopted by a wide variety of practice orientations (e.g., see Schneider, 2008; Stolorow, Brandschaft, & Atwood, 1987). Still, the expansion and diversification of existential therapy are a relatively recent phenomenon, because it has historically been practiced in white, middle- to upper-class neighborhoods with white, middle- to upper-class clients. There is, however, no necessary link between such clientele and effective psychotherapy. The benefits of presence, I–Thou encounter, and responsibility are cross-cultural and cross-disciplinary (May, 1972; Rice, 2008; Vontress & Epp, 2001).

In short, there is considerable ecumenism in contemporary E–H practice. This ecumenism is characterized by cross-disciplinary openness, adaptations for diverse populations, and sliding fee scales. In the end, no formulaic guideline determines the course of E–H therapy. Each client and therapist pair—each humanity—must have its say.

Still, E–H therapy, even of the integrative variety, has specific problems as well as advantages. One of the problems of E–H therapy is its tendency to invite depth and intensity where circumstances may or may not call for such (Cooper, 2004). For example, within the existential–integrative model of practice, clients whose desire and capacity for change are highly delimited (e.g., due to psychological fragility, cultural outlook, and intellectual acuity) may not benefit from the fuller, experiential phases of that approach (Schneider, 2008). By the same token, clients who seek short-term, symptom-reducing therapy probably will not appreciate lengthy or intensive opportunities to anatomize their life concerns. On the other hand, a signal advantage of E–H therapy, particularly of the integrative variety, is that should ostensibly short-term clients change or respond unexpectedly to the E–H experiential field, intensive, longer-term exploration may be just what they ultimately require.

In sum, there is no cardinal rule about for whom or in what circumstances E–H therapy will prove most effective. In keeping with the E–H practice philosophy, each connection, each setting, and indeed, each moment must be carefully and mindfully appraised. Again, we cannot say enough about the value of presence for assessing the appropriateness of E–H (or any other kind of) therapy for struggling, panicking lives. To the extent that therapists can draw on their whole-bodied experience in therapy, they will be in an enhanced position to relate to, assess, and serve the clients they engage.

HOW DOES E–H THERAPY WORK WITH DIVERSE CLIENTS?

E–H therapy is evolving successfully with a wide variety of client populations. The research on the effectiveness of common factors or contextual dimensions of therapy also upholds the value of a comprehensive E–H approach (Elkins, 2007; Wampold, 2001, 2008). The issue for E–H therapy is not so much the background of a given client, but the meaning of that background for clients' living, unfolding experience. People's living, unfolding experience, in other words, may or may not conform to their demographic profile, and while it is important to account for that profile, it is abasement, in our view, to overestimate its role. The chief question is, What is the client's desire and capacity for change, and how can the therapeutic experience best mobilize, support, and help to unleash that desire and capacity? This is the E–H therapist's charge.

Consider, for example, the existentially oriented case study of an African American client, Darrin, by Donadrian Rice (2008). After a "breakdown of rapport" between Darrin and his former white therapist, who attributed Darrin's depression to "overwork," Darrin sought counseling from Dr. Rice, an African American existential therapist. By attuning to Darrin's immediate socioeconomic plight, helping him to manage his debts, and supporting him to develop choice, Rice was able to assist Darrin to reflect more substantively on his life, not merely his pocketbook. In a parallel vein, the existential case of Mariana, by Lillian Comas-Diaz (2008), incorporated what Comas-Diaz called "Latin-American humanism" and "Latino psychospirituality" (p. 100). By these terms, Comas-Diaz meant a "wisdom"—"Sabiduria"—that connects spiritual development with healing (p. 101). By presiding by Mariana with the aforementioned sensibilities, Comas-Diaz was able to support her to rediscover both the tragedy and opportunity in an ancestral trauma and to rediscover her roots—as well as herself—through art. "Therapy helped me to become an artist of life," Mariana proclaimed at the conclusion of the study (p. 107).

These examples notwithstanding, much more research is needed to deepen our understanding of the salience of E–H offerings. We need to know more specifically how presence, invoking the actual, working with resistance or protections, and the cultivation of meaning and awe affect clients from diverse backgrounds with diverse needs. Vontress and Epp (2001) emphasize the point:

> Existential cross-cultural counseling is a rich philosophical approach to psychotherapy that shares many of the same tenets with the world's major cultures and religions . . . It is this fact that makes it a universally applicable theory of counseling. However, existentialism also challenges the other counseling perspectives in its expansive view of life . . . and its belief that a narrow focus on cognitions, feelings, or psychodynamics in the therapeutic relationship addresses only a narrow slice of existence. Ultimately, the existential cross-cultural counselor wishes to concertedly explore with the client all of life; not simply the random issues that emerge in the session . . . (p. 386)

A Note About the Social and Spiritual
Dimensions of E–H Transformation

The quote from Vontress and Epp brings into focus a major critique of psychotherapy in recent years. This criticism comprises three main points: (a) that psychotherapy is overly individualized; (b) that it feeds a materialist, consumerist mind-set; and (c) that it is politically naïve or regressive (Cushman, 1995; Hillman & Ventura, 1992). "We have had 100 years of psychotherapy," Hillman and Ventura (1992) inveigh, "and the world's getting worse."

The question, however, is which *form* of psychotherapy the detractors are targeting and whose particular world is "getting worse." Although Hillman and Ventura appear to include E–H therapy in their generalized indictment, is this inclusion warranted? From an E–H point of view, for example, there is certainly merit to the problem of a worsening world. In many quarters of the globe, class divisiveness and materialist ambition appear to be on the rise, whereas, at the same time, conviviality, interethnic understanding, and magnanimity appear to be waning. But is E–H practice among the instigators of these developments? We would reply both yes and no. "Yes" in the sense that it is sometimes overly individualistic, but "no" in the sense that it has consistently opposed the simplistic, cosmetic, and mechanical in therapeutic conduct, which are the primary corrosive influences in our view (e.g., see Laing, 1967; May, 1983).

In any case, one point has become increasingly clear: One cannot simply heal individuals to the neglect of the social context within which they are thrust. To be a responsible practitioner, one must develop a vision of responsible social change, alongside of and in coordination with one's vision of individual transformation—and increasingly, E–H practitioners are becoming conscious of this interdependence (Mendelowitz, 2001, 2008; O'Hara, 2001; Pierson & Sharp, 2001).

The question is one of social advocacy: On whose behalf does a therapist function—the culture, the institutional norm, the conventions of the health care industry, or the client? While none of these can be neglected from an E–H point of view, it is emphatically the client, and the profound subjective and intersubjective realizations of depth-experiential inquiry, that reflect the chief priority of E–H therapy. This person-centered priority, moreover, is not just for the revitalization of individuals, it is for the revitalization of their (our) community, culture, and indeed, world (e.g., see Buber, 1970; Bugental & Bracke, 1992; Friedman, 2001; Hanna, Giordano, Dupuy, & Puhakka, 1995; and May, 1981). To put it another way, E–H therapy promotes depth inquiry, and depth inquiry promotes a sense of what deeply matters. While such a sense does not always lead to social and spiritual consciousness, in our experience—and that of many E–H practitioners—this is predominantly what results.

6

Future Developments

The problems with market-driven health care—or the "quick-fix" model for living—are mounting (Cushman, 1995; Kuhl, 1994; Schneider, 2005). Yet approaches such as existential–humanistic (E–H) therapy, which prize the *person* of the client, provide a hedge against this intensifying trend. This is not to say that E–H therapists deny the periodic need for expedience in the facilitation of therapeutic healing. As we have taken pains to point out in this volume, E–H therapists increasingly appreciate such practicality, but—and this is key—only within the context of a more holistic availability. For example, E–H therapists are circumspect about "treating" a client as a medical doctor "treats" a patient, or a pharmacist gives a patient a remedy. At the same time, E–H therapists recognize that there are moments, such as in emergencies, when clients both seek and need such guidance from therapy, and it should be implemented accordingly. The key point here, however, is that therapy does not generally end with such moments, and that opportunities for clients to develop agency (meaning, depth, alignment with what matters) are critical.

While remedies in the medical sense may be seductive, and even helpful, initially, they can also prove, as suggested previously, notoriously short-lived. Consider the conclusion of Wampold (2001), after an exhaustive analysis of the literature:

> Therapy practice is both a science and an art. . . . [T]he master therapist, informed by psychological knowledge and theory and guided by experience, produces an artistry that assists clients to move ahead in their lives with meaning and health. Treating clients as if they were medical patients receiving mandated treatments conducted with manuals . . . stifle[s] the artistry. (p. 225)

E–H therapy, in our view, is at the forward edge of the movement to which Wampold alludes—the melding of art and science, evidence and experience. The question is, Can E–H therapy lead this movement into the coming era? This question is crucial because the frame we use to integrate practice will have profound effects on the public we serve. For example, if cognitive–behavioral therapy is the context within which we incorporate other therapeutic modes, then the context of clients' healing will be bound by cognitive–behavioral techniques, principles, and goals.

We contend that E–H therapy should be a leading context within which integrative practices are utilized. Consider, for a moment, what an E–H integration of practice is likely to instill: the enhancement of presence, both to oneself as therapist and to one's client; the value of this enhancement for the understanding and support of the therapeutic process; the clarification of clients' core struggles; the elucidation of the blocks to that clarification; and finally, the enabling of access to clients' range of possibilities for a poignant and meaningful life. What clients would not benefit from such opportunities? What therapists would not appreciate the benefits that such opportunities can bring?

Some of the newer branches of E–H practice that we would like to see pursued include the EI (existential–integrative) model we have discussed in this volume as well as specific integrations of practice in the areas of multiculturalism (Comas-Diaz, 2008; Rice, 2008; Vontress, 2001), gender identity (Brown, 2008; Monheit, 2008; Serlin, 2008), sexual abuse (Fisher, 2005), psychoses (Dorman, 2008; Thompson, 1995), religion and spirituality (Bowman, 1995; Bradford, 2007; Hoffman, 2008), cognitive–behavioral therapy (Bunting & Hayes, 2008; Wolfe, 2008), and psychodynamic and relational modalities (Fosha 2008; Krug, 2009; Portnoy, 2008; Stolorow, 2008).

We also encourage the continued development of E–H therapy in the areas of group encounter for the elderly (E. Bugental, 2008), supportive therapy for returning war veterans (Decker, 2007; Krippner & Paulson, 2007), and arts-based therapy for the emotionally and physically disabled (Serlin, 2007; Serlin & Marcow Speiser, 2007). Finally, we encourage the further elaboration of E–H theory with respect to aspects of "the self," identity formation, and therapeutic change (Krug & Goulet, 2009).

OUTLOOK AND CHALLENGES

The outlook for E–H therapy is both guarded and hopeful. It is guarded to the extent that all depth therapies are guarded and under threat today—by an encroaching ethos of standardization. Moreover, as students, instructors, and professional organizations acquiesce to, and in some cases encourage, that ethos, there is a decreasing incentive to teach and apply E–H alternatives (Bohart et al., 1997; Schneider, 1998a, 1999b).

On the other hand, the outlook for the future is not so one-sided as it may seem. As previously suggested, there are trends, such as the embrace of experientially informed practice, that run directly counter to the aforementioned scenario. These trends suggest that a backlash is building and that E–H therapy is on its cutting edge, as is holistic and integrative medicine, comprehensive health care, and social and spiritual activism (e.g., see Criswell, 2001; Elkins, 2001; Lyons, 2001; Montouri & Purser, 2001; Schneider, 1998a, 2004; Serlin, 2007).

As E–H therapy evolves, moreover, it is converging with other "liberation-based" therapies. These therapies are influencing the culture beyond the traditional two-person context. Drawing on E–H practice principles, for example, O'Hara (2001) has elaborated an ever-widening E–H application. She documents the use of E–H approaches in the schools, business community, and human service fields and pleads for a society-wide E–H reformation.

Finally, what Schneider (2004, 2009) has termed the "awe-based" in psychology is an attempt to apply existential-depth principles to a variety of social arenas—from childrearing to education and from the work setting to religion and government. Others, such as gang mediator and former gang leader James Hernandez, are furthering this awe-based approach directly. Hernandez is spearheading a project for the Ernest Becker Foundation of Seattle, Washington, to bring awe-based principles of practice to his work with violent and troubled youth ("Assisting Youth," 2007). Such communalization of practice is critical in our view, if society is to both mature and flourish.

To the extent that these trends continue—and there is reason for optimism that they will (e.g., Ray, 1996)—then correlative trends should also grow, such as funding for E–H practices, support for E–H training, and investment in E–H theory building.

On the other hand, we do not want to sound glib about the difficulties E–H and related practice modalities face in the coming years. Managed care, programmatic mental health practices, and medicalization are here to stay, and there are sound bases for their existence. But what we do wish to emphasize is that with discernment, focus, and passion, a major transformation can be staged in psychotherapy. This change will not be exclusivist, and it will not reject conventional modalities, but it will widen, deepen, and integrate these modalities, and it will weave them into a liberating whole.

Summary

This book has examined the history, theoretical framework, and practical application of contemporary existential–humanistic (E–H) therapy. Deeply rooted in the question of what it means to be fully and subjectively alive, E–H therapy is an amalgam of approaches that emphasize experiential liberation and transformation.

BACKGROUND

Beginning in the late 1950s, E–H therapy became an established therapeutic orientation. With the advent of Rollo May's Existence (1958) and culminating in James Bugental's Search for Authenticity (1965), E–H therapy took its place alongside the three major practice orientations of the era—psychoanalysis, behaviorism, and client-centered therapy. Yet E–H therapy also departed from all three orientations on the basis of a radically new outlook—at least for America. This outlook emphasized freedom, experiential reflection, and responsibility. While psychoanalysis advocated freedom (albeit in a restricted form), it lacked the stress on "whole bodied," experiential reflection; and while it supported ego development, it lacked an accent on personal responsibility. Behaviorism, meanwhile, lacked almost any emphasis on freedom, experiential reflection, and responsibility and wedded its philosophy to conditioning. Client-centered therapy came closest to E–H therapy in its aims—and shared its humanistic philosophy—but lacked its intensity, particularly in the area of personal and interpersonal struggle.

May and Bugental thus augmented these aforementioned trends within American therapy with vigorous new practice modalities that added concreteness, intensity, philosophical depth (imported mainly from Europe), and spiritual breadth. Among the modalities elaborated were presence, authenticity, and will.

By the 1980s Irvin Yalom consolidated his predecessors' therapeutic outlook with an accessible, highly scholarly guide called *Existential Psychotherapy* (1980). This text has helped to make E–H therapy more comprehendible to a diversity of practitioners. With its focus on the "givens" of existence—death, freedom, isolation, and meaninglessness—and its emphasis on relationship to negotiate them, Yalom's perspective gave E–H therapy a "map." Maurice Friedman (1991a, 1991b, 1995, 2001), too, embellished on this map with his evocation of Martin Buber's I-Thou philosophy. Like Yalom, Friedman emphasized "healing through meeting" as the chief therapeutic wedge.

THE PRESENT SITUATION

By the 1990s, E–H therapy began yet another evolution in the form of integrative methodology. In their 1995 book, *The Psychology of Existence*, Kirk Schneider and Rollo May assessed the shortcomings of rarified forms of E–H practice, along with proliferating managed care policies, and set about to reinvigorate both. With the advent of existential–integrative (EI) therapy—updated by Schneider in 2008—Schneider and May drew inspiration from May's original, prophetic stance:

> [E–H therapy] does not purport to found a new school . . . over against other schools or to give a new technique of therapy . . . [but] seeks rather to analyze the structure of human existence . . . which if successful, should yield an understanding of the reality underlying all situations of human beings in crisis. (May, 1958a, p. 7)

Hence by setting forth one way to coordinate a variety of therapeutic modalities within an overarching existential or experiential context, EI therapy became a new bridge to both mainstream and existentially oriented therapies. This new bridge offered fresh cross-fertilizations of knowledge and expanded repertoires of practice. As a result, today's E–H therapy has for many become an integrative therapy, impacting diverse clinical and socioeconomic needs.

THE INCREASING RESEARCH SUPPORT FOR E–H THERAPY

As can be seen in this volume, there is a striking upsurge in empirical support for E–H therapy. Studies, from therapy outcome to neurology, from clinical training to psychiatric care, show convincingly that E–H therapy is on to something critical for the viability of our profession. This critical factor appears to associate with the personal and interpersonal dimensions of therapy—presence, experiential encounter, and mobilization of will. Without these dimensions—incidental or intended—healing is compromised. With them, on the other hand, healing is facilitated.

Recent research, moreover, shows that personal and interpersonal factors, not therapeutic techniques, are primarily responsible for positive therapeutic outcome. To the extent that these factors are at the core of E–H practice, we propose that students who have specific training in E–H therapy will likely be more capable of effecting therapeutic change.

The outlook for E–H therapy is encouraging but guarded. In addition to developing integrative modalities, E–H therapy is also fostering new relationships to the world. For example, the Existential–Humanistic Institute and the International Institute for Humanistic Studies, both in the San Francisco Bay Area, are disseminating E–H practices to a growing regional and worldwide audience. Among the countries benefiting from trainings by these institutes (or their instructors) are Russia, Lithuania, Poland, Japan, and China (the first major U.S.–China existential therapy conference is slated for April, 2010). Younger E–H theorists, such as Louis Hoffman at the University of the Rockies and Shawn Rubin at the Michigan School of Professional Psychology, have been actively introducing students to the new E–H practice philosophies, and women, such as Orah Krug, Elizabeth Bugental, and Myrtle Heery, have been advancing a new feminist sensibility in E–H theory and practice.

In short, there is no end to which E–H practice philosophies are being applied today, and the surge of energy around this approach is palpable. (See Hoffman, Yang, Kakluaskas, & Chan, 2009, and Hoffman, Stewart, Warren, & Meek, 2009, for comprehensive overviews of existential psychology's diverse and growing influence.) That said, it remains to be seen whether and how E–H advocates will be received in the coming years, given societal trends. While these trends show signs of increasing openness to E–H sensibilities, they also, as previously noted, show signs of quashing those sensibilities or converting them for expediency.

CONCLUSION

To achieve the aims of E–H therapy, practitioners draw on a variety of means. These means, however, are not techniques in the classical sense; they are stances (or conditions) through which experiential liberation *and* profound transformation can take root. Among the core intertwining and overlapping E–H stances are the following: the cultivation of therapeutic presence (presence as ground); the cultivation and activation of therapeutic presence through struggle (presence as method and goal); the encounter with the resistance to therapeutic struggle; and the coalescence of the meaning, intentionality, and life awakening (awe) that can result from the struggle. Although E–H therapy converges on these themes, their expression and the manner in which they are facilitated are contextual. Each therapist, and therapist–client pair, must rediscover what is optimal, and each moment can signal what can be optimized. This is the art—and emerging science—of contemporary E–H practice.

Short-Term Case 2: Hamilton

The following case draws upon Kirk Schneider's (2008) existential–integrative (EI) approach to therapy. EI therapy coordinates a variety of therapeutic approaches (e.g., physiological, environmental, cognitive, psychoanalytic, and experiential) within an overarching existential or experiential context.

EI therapy is exemplified in Schneider's work with Hamilton, a 28-year-old, white, married salesperson with acrophobia, a fear of heights. Although Hamilton had a circumscribed concern, acrophobia, and was mainly interested in "curing" that concern within the parameters of his 16-session HMO plan, he was also open to finding out more about his life and the potential connections that could be made for his overall health. In deference to Hamilton's main focus, but also acknowledging his openness to exploration, I worked with him along an interweaving path. On the one hand, I worked with him to alleviate his phobia, and on the other, I assisted him to be present to spontaneously emerging material. This stance is not atypical for E–H practitioners. With clients who exhibit well-delineated problems, E–H practitioners find ways to address those problems while at the same time remaining open to the deeper contexts within which those problems arise (e.g., Wolfe, 2008).

In Hamilton's case, I explained to him my interweaving approach and contracted with him to begin the process with a modified application of systematic desensitization and in vivo exposure. This kind of preparatory communication (or "psychoeducation") is often helpful, particularly within brief formats, to mobilize clients' capacities for change (J. Bugental, 2008). It is also helpful within such settings to set relatively clear objectives and to confine expectations to realistic parameters (J. Bugental, 2008). In accord with this latter axiom, I proceeded cautiously with Hamilton, neither overestimating nor underestimating his ability to deepen therapeutic awareness.

Put another way, I attempted to remain as attuned as possible to Hamilton's desire and capacity for experiential change, or change that is felt and lived not just adopted. The desire and capacity for change, in my view, is a key bellwether of integrative existential practice. It has two basic functions: (a) it signals to therapists when and with what degree of intensity clients can be therapeutically engaged, and (b) it guides therapists in the selection of appropriate liberation conditions for those engagements. Among the liberation conditions available are nonexperiential modalities, such as those of cognitive behaviorism; semi-experiential modalities, such as those of psychoanalysis; and experiential modalities, such as those associated with existential humanism (Schneider, 2008).

Within our desensitization-experiential focus, I interwove all three liberation conditions with Hamilton. Given his desire and capacity for delimited change, I emphasized the cognitive–behavioral offering but weaved in and out, as warranted, with both semi-experiential and experiential offerings, challenging him to deepen his newly conditioned responses.

We began our work, accordingly, with a discussion of and preparation for systematic desensitization. Gradually and at his pace, I assisted Hamilton to develop an anxiety hierarchy and to pair deep relaxation with ever-intensifying visualizations of his phobia (Wolpe, 1969). Hamilton began the exercise with a visualization of waking up on the day he was about to climb the steps of a tall building (a feat he had recently, but unsuccessfully, attempted). Next, I assisted him to pair relaxation (diaphragmatic breathing) with that very first image. After he was able to fully relax into that image, I then helped him to pair relaxation with a visualization of himself approaching the target building. We then worked with his entrance into the building, and so on.

After about 3 weeks, we were ready for the next critical encounter with his anxiety hierarchy—the visualization of his ascent to the top of my building, about five stories high. We delicately approached this stage, which we both knew he would attempt to enact, by combining systematic desensitization skills with periodic explorations of his anxiety. Hence, as the moment warranted, I would gently invite Hamilton, not just to report about his feelings as he was visualizing, say, climbing the stairs to the fifth floor landing, but to stay present to those feelings and to associate to related feelings, sensations, and images as they arose. At times this exercise yielded minimal responsiveness from Hamilton, but at other times, he expressed vivid and bountiful impressions, from a childhood stumble on a playground, to a shaky moment on a bridge. But the percepts became even more subtle.

On one occasion, for example, he envisioned a churning in his stomach area, which then led to a memory of sitting with his grandmother when he was very small. The details were sketchy, but what he remembered most was that his grandmother was sobbing and his mother was deathly ill. He also remembered feeling utterly alone in that moment and terrified that he would be abandoned. I invited Hamilton to stay present to that moment and see what other feelings, sensations, or images might emerge. His face reddened and he began to tear up. Fear was his main feeling and the sense that he could not fill the hole of his parental longing, his sense of being left.

After encouraging Hamilton to stay with his painful affects for a period, he was able to enter a renewed, if temporary, sense of solidity. At this point we agreed to continue working with his anxiety hierarchy and gradually progressed toward his target goal. We spent a number of other sessions on similar shifts between desensitization conditioning and periodic explorations of affect. We talked about emergent material and worked with him to stay present to the here-and-now experience of that material. In time, and at the point where we both felt he was ready, I accompanied Hamilton up the five flights of stairs to the top of my well-secured and accessible landing. I frequently checked in with Hamilton as we ascended and provided him with ample moments to stop and practice his breathing exercises. To our mutual gratification, Hamilton felt surprisingly positive at virtually each point along the ascent. When we arrived at the top, I checked in with Hamilton one more time and suggested that he practice his relaxation response. He did so and then raised his head to the level of the vista spread out before us. Slowly and somewhat anxiously, he began to survey the scene. As he did so, I checked in with him about his experience, which was generally quite stable. Over time we made five ascents to this landing, and each one became progressively easier for Hamilton. In between ascents, we would continue to integrate desensitization with here-and-now exploration and would embellish on this regimen, though in modified form, at the top of the landing.

After each trip up the stairs, we would return to the consulting room and debrief. Hamilton and I agreed, that after 16 weeks, he underwent a significant transformation. Not only was he freer to ascend heights, both in my building and in his life in general, he was freer with his feelings and his ability to communicate. By the time we ended therapy, it seemed to me—as well as to Hamilton—that he had assimilated parts of himself that he had long shut away and that cultivating presence seeded a new intrapersonal relationship. He seemed to feel more centered in himself and less edgy, more aware, and less threatened. It also seemed that the groundlessness that Hamilton experienced as a child and that still clearly reverberated in his life bore a significant relationship to his anxiety on steep physical structures. While systematic reconditioning removed some of this anguish, working with him to "reoccupy" himself, to live through his most dreaded recollections, appeared to add a fresh dimension. This dimension was evident as a general sense of robustness in his life. He gained more energy, became more decisive, and felt more assured. It was as if he "grew up" a very young part of himself during the course of our brief work. Both literally and figuratively, he became a larger presence, and that presence had salutary effects.

In closing, although Hamilton made critical gains over the course of our existential–integrative work, it is not at all clear how long those gains would endure. The most E–H therapists can say about shorter-term mediation is that it can provide a highly beneficial tool or staging ground for continued life-growth (J. Bugental, 2008; Galvin, 2008). The question as to whether this growth can be sustained by the client, or will require adjunctive facilitation is a function of both the depth of the client's suffering and her or his means or capacity to maximally redress that suffering.

Summary of Experiential Stances of the Existential–Integrative (EI) Model

The following is an outline of the experiential level of contact of the existential–integration (EI) model as demonstrated in this volume (see also Schneider, 2008).

OVERVIEW

The general idea of EI therapy is to assist clients to optimize choice (freedom) within the natural and self-imposed (i.e., cultural) limitations of living. Choice is characterized by the capacity to constrict and expand as the person and situation demand. Although choice always entails will, it does not have to be willful; it can, if a person is so inclined, reflect deliberate decisions to "give up" one's will or to stay present to that which impels one.

The client's desire and capacity for change is the key determinant of choice. Desire and capacity for change are derivative of clients' and therapists' dispositions. To the degree that therapists are open and available to clients for deeper contact, clients too, within their unique parameters, become maximally open and available. Generally the greater clients' desires and capacities for change, the more they can become present to themselves and the more they can "occupy" the denied poles of their (self–world) existence. Through occupying the poles of their existence, clients can discover themselves and roam within, as it were, to live as richly, poignantly, and fully as the designs of their lives will permit.

Based on material from Kirk Schneider (2008, pp. 89–90).

The following are stances or conditions of the experiential (i.e., imme-diate, affective, kinesthetic, and profound) level of contact within the EI model. These stances often, but not necessarily, proceed sequentially.

Presence

Presence holds and illuminates that which is palpably (immediately, affectively, kinesthetically, and profoundly) relevant within the client and between client and therapist. Presence holds and illuminates that which is charged and implies the question, What is really going on here within the person and between the person and me? Presence is the "soup," the atmosphere within which a struggle or battle becomes clarified.

Invoking the Actual

Invoking the actual is helping the client into that which is palpably relevant or charged. Put another way, it calls attention to the part of the client that is attempting to emerge. Invoking the actual is characterized (though not exhausted) by the following:

- Topical focus, as in questions such as "What's of concern?" "What really matters right now?" "Where are you at?"
- Personal focus, as in encouraging "I" statements or statements in the first-person; staying present to what really matters at a given moment; or giving a concrete example.
- Topical expansion, as in questions and invitations such as "Can you tell me more?" "Stay with that feeling for a moment." "Try slowing down."
- Attention to process as much or more than content, as in attending to the preverbal/kinesthetic way clients talk and hold themselves, their vocal fluctuations and breathing, and attention to process/content dis-crepancies such as "I hear your serious words, and yet you laugh."
- Embodied meditation, or concerted attention to body sensations, often accompanied by invitations to clients to place their hand on areas noted, such as tension areas or areas that feel blocked, and by follow-up invi-tations to associate any other feelings, sensations, or images to these aforementioned areas.

- Interpersonal encounter, or attention to charged themes in the living therapeutic relationship; attention to process dimensions of themes; pursuing and exploring the associations to those dimensions; and mutuality as facilitative of client self-exploration.

Vivifying and Confronting Resistance (Protections)

Vivifying resistance is *alerting* clients about how they block palpably relevant material. Vivifying resistance is exemplified by noting and tagging points at which clients diverge from or suppress emotionally charged material. Confronting resistance, on the other hand, is intended to *alarm* clients about how they block palpably relevant material. Confronting resistance must be cautiously engaged. If confrontation is too harsh, it can retraumatize clients; if it is ill-timed, it can prompt destructive backlashes or, conversely, passive dependency. Both vivifying and confronting help clients to "see" close-up how they construct their worlds and implicitly challenge clients to make a decision about those worlds. Put another way, resistance work holds a mirror to the side of the client that is attempting to keep herself or himself in the familiar yet debilitating pattern of the past. By implication it builds the counterwill (or frustration) necessary for the client to overcome her or his blocks.

Rediscovery of Meaning and Awe

As clients overcome the blocks to that which deeply matters in their lives, they begin to develop new, more aligned life paths. As these paths solidify, clients often experience the freedom to embrace life itself—in all its stark possibility. This new relationship to life, being, or the mystery of creation is often characterized by awe—the humility and wonder, or thrill and anxiety of living. (See Schneider, 2004, 2009, for an elaboration on the rediscovery of awe.)

Phases of Change in a "Typical" Long-Term Existential Therapy

What follows is a model developed to help explain how and why we focus on the unfolding process to cultivate intra- and interpersonal presence. This model arbitrarily divides the therapeutic journey into three phases, although in reality the journey is never as linear or concrete. Therapy is, in fact, a circular and reiterative process. Accordingly, in approaching this model, remember that the model is not the experience, simply a crude attempt to abstract the complex and vital experience of the therapist and client. Each phase of change describes: (a) the ways in which the client is typically present, (b) the therapeutic goal, (c) the problem and challenge, (d) the process to resolve the problem, and (e) the typical outcome.

PHASE ONE

Typically Present: Anxiety

Goal: To develop an intimate therapeutic relationship and to help the client have "I am" experiences; that is, "I am aware that I exist and that to some extent I am willing to take responsibility for the life that I have."

Problem: Twofold: (a) without a sense of safety and security, the client will not be able to do his or her work, and (b) a client's sense of self is typically repressed, which results in constricted and/or fragmented sense of self. Anxiety signals that adjustment is breaking down. There exists in

---

The structure of this model is based on several chapters in May's classic text (1983) and on Bugental's (1978, pp. 92–100) phases of therapy—but mostly it is based on 30 years of therapeutic collaboration with my clients, whose courage to grow and change never ceases to inspire. The phases of change are illustrated in Appendix D, which presents a case study of a client, Claudia.

the client a potential for reconstituting her or his sense of self and world if the therapist can create a safe and intimate therapeutic relationship.

Process: Therapist encounters client with deep presence and empathy, focusing on both intra- and interpersonal dynamics—attending to the client's concrete ways of being and relating, such as her or his posture, voice, behaviors, and assumptions. The intention is twofold: (a) to create a safe and intimate therapeutic relationship and (b) to illuminate what is immediate but unnoticed in the living moment. The cultivation of intra- and interpersonal presence is essential to help the client identify her or his blocks or life-limiting patterns of behavior that function to keep the client safe but that are ultimately restrictive. The therapist may use dreams as well as spoken metaphors to further facilitate this process.

Outcome: The client, feeling safe, takes a more active stance in therapy, becomes more engaged in the therapeutic process, and assumes appropriate responsibility for creating her or his life-limiting patterns of behavior. Client experiences a limited amount of personal freedom: "I can choose how to be."

PHASE TWO

Typically Present: Willingness
The client feels sufficiently safe and secure in the therapeutic relationship; client and therapist are an effective collaborative team.

Goal: To discover deeper levels of "I am" (intentionality) to effect real and lasting change.

Problem: "I am" experiences are only the prerequisite for change. The client needs to move from awareness and responsibility to action. A client's awareness of her or his intentionality is usually needed for this to happen—that is, "I understand that I continually create meanings about my self and my world, I make choices based on these meanings, and I act accordingly, therefore, 'I am.'"

Process: The encounter is focused primarily on illuminating deeper levels of subjective experience often using dreams and the searching process for this purpose. The focus is on removing the blocks interfering with the ability to wish, want, and act.

Outcome: The client is more conscious of her or his intentionality. There is increased willingness to face existential givens and an increased desire for meaning and purpose. The client experiences an expanded sense of self through action. She or he is in the process of reforming a sense of identity, of self and world.

PHASE THREE

Typically Present: Creativity
The client experiences expanded self and relational presence.

Goal: To fulfill the evolutionary task of creative engagement. Dissolve the client's blocks or life-limiting patterns so that the client can realize greater possibilities and have a deeper sense of meaning and purpose in her or his life.

Problem: Expanded consciousness and expanded sense of self is only the first of a two-part process. The second part involves creatively engaging in the world. The client needs to actualize her or his potentialities within the givens of her or his life.

Process: Therapist supports, cultivates, and nurtures newly emerging self-actualizing attitudes, behaviors, and actions, working with the client intra- and interpersonally to focus on blocks or barriers to enacting potentialities.

Outcome: Expanded consciousness, expanded sense of self and self-actualizing experiences. The client experiences a greater capacity to love and work. Client can creatively engage in her or his life with meaning and purpose.

APPENDIX D

Long-Term Case 2: Claudia

When a new client walks into my therapy room, I am often aware of the fact that neither of us has any idea of what paths we will travel or how long our journey will be. That, for me, is one of the fascinating aspects of this work.

When "Claudia" walked into my office, I could not have foreseen the intense and challenging path on which we were about embark, a path that would significantly affect our lives and change us both. Fifteen minutes into our first session, however, Claudia gave me a clue about what the focus of our work would be. She looked right at me for the first time and seemed to search my face for an answer to her question, "Are you the one I can trust to help me?" It has been suggested that a client reveals all of her or his issues in the first hour. As an existential therapist, I essentially accept that premise, assuming as I do that the past is alive in some way in the present moment. As she searched my face, Claudia seemed to be saying, "I want help but I'm afraid to trust." At the time I did not know the full extent of her desire to be known and her fear of that happening. We came to understood that her conflict was both intra- and interpersonal in nature, one that we would revisit many times throughout our work together.

Claudia came to therapy ostensibly to decide if she should move forward in a relationship with a man with whom she had been living for several years. At the time, Claudia was a 29-year-old, single woman, recently unemployed, and uncertain about her career path. She was financially independent as a result of a substantial trust fund set up by her mother and father, who owned a successful commercial real estate company in the South. Unlike her two younger brothers who worked in the family business,

---

Case study presented by Orah Krug.

Claudia showed no interest in following in her parents' footsteps. In fact, Claudia seemed as lost with respect to what she wanted to do in her life as she was about her relationship.

In the first few sessions, I noted that Claudia's "lostness" was related to her lack of connection to her inner experience. This manifested in several ways. She typically observed herself from the outside, treating herself like an object to be analyzed. She talked very fast and low as if she really didn't want me to hear what she was saying. At the start of each session, she would curl her petite frame into a ball on my couch, remaining that way throughout, looking rarely at me but out the window. This is why in our first session when she unexpectedly searched my face for an answer to her question, she caught my attention. She had difficulty making "I" statements and typically talked about herself in the third person, carefully editing everything she communicated and often laughing afterward to diminish the impact of her statement.

Her trust issues emerged more concretely in our second session as she related how her first great love had abruptly left her without any explanation. She was hurt and confused by his actions and has had difficulty trusting other men's expressions of love and affection since then. I asked her if she was generally mistrustful of people's intentions. She hesitated and then looked at me and nodded yes.

OK: Perhaps you're aware of having difficulty trusting me right now? Claudia nods.

OK: How is it to tell me this?

Claudia: I'm afraid I've hurt your feelings.

OK: Do you want to ask me something about that?

Claudia [gathering her courage]: Have I?

OK: Not at all. Most people have difficulty trusting their therapist when they begin. I know I did. After all, you don't know me yet. I must demonstrate my trustworthiness to you. Our goal is to build a relationship in which you feel safe and accepted. This takes time because it takes time to build trust.

Claudia seemed to relax after hearing this. A little later I had an opportunity to share with her my understanding of our collaborative effort. I told her it means that I will often focus on our relationship, as I did earlier, to find out what is happening between. I asked her if this way of working was okay with her, and she said yes. Phase One of our therapy had begun, as I focused Claudia on our relationship and created opportunities for her to be present to herself and present to me in our relationship.

We met once a week for about 1 year. During that time, I attempted to have Claudia experience the ways in which her "lost" feelings were perpetuated by her constant self-analysis. When I tried to teach her how to slow down, make space, and search within, she became agitated or reported that there was nothing there. She was clearly uncomfortable connecting subjectively. She was in her comfort zone when reporting about herself as a neutral, outside observer. She could "talk about" feeling stupid and unlovable but never allowed herself to experience those feelings in the moment. It seemed imperative that she keep herself disconnected from her feelings so that she wouldn't know in an experiential way that something mattered or that she hurt. When she was not being "neutral," she was being critical. Her harsh internal critic constantly berated her for not doing something right. For example, she was mad at herself for always yielding to her boyfriend's wishes, but she felt unable to change, believing as she did that he would leave and there would be no one else because she was such a loser. It struck me that Claudia's voice was like a harsh prison guard speaking to an unruly prisoner. My mirroring that back to her didn't seem to help her silence the voice, no matter how many times I pointed it out.

Something was obviously blocking Claudia from being compassionate with herself and from believing in her worth and value. As Claudia revealed her family history, I began to understand why. Claudia's family looked great on paper, an intact, church-going family whose parents, Charles and Renee, were fabulously successful business partners as well as marriage partners. But behind the scenes, things were less rosy. Charles was a distant and domineering husband and father. He ruled the household as he ran his business—demanding perfection and instilling fear in those around him. He was quick to anger and would verbally and sometimes physically abuse his children. Renee once confided to Claudia that she knew he'd had a number of affairs, but as she told her daughter, she kept quiet because she was afraid he would leave if she confronted him. Renee presented a picture of a powerful and successful businesswoman. But Claudia sensed her mother's unhappiness and insecurity. Claudia tried to be a "good girl," hoping this would make her mother happy and keep her under her mother's "radar." But Renee was not maternal and had little patience for her children.

To say that as a child Claudia's feelings, wants, and wishes went unacknowledged would be a huge understatement. Outwardly her childhood was a dream come true, a beautiful home, lots of clothes, and the best schools, but inwardly there was little to nurture her. Claudia grew up feeling unloved and uncared for, lonely and scared. Moreover, she consistently questioned her talents and abilities because they went unnoticed by her parents. But I still wondered after a year of therapy why Claudia was so disconnected from her feelings.

She had made some progress that year, as she decided to break up with her boyfriend even though it scared her and as she began to explore what she really wanted to do in her life. Shyly she told me about her passion for art and photography. As a child she walked around with a drawing pad and pencil in hand, sketching everything in sight. At age 14, she bought a camera and began taking photo portraits of friends and people on the street. Although she loved her creative side, she constantly shoved it to one side, telling herself she wasn't good enough to make a career of it. Neither of her parents valued her talent although many teachers recognized it and vigorously encouraged her to pursue it. Instead, she did as her parents wanted. She majored in business, with a minor in art, and then got her MBA. After graduate school, she worked at a large company for 2 years but disliked the corporate environment and the work.

Even though she knew she didn't want to work in the corporate world, she nevertheless had great difficulty imagining that she could have a career in a more artistically oriented world. Her dream was to be a portrait photographer, but she had difficulty sharing her artistic desires, hopes, and dreams with me. Each time she tried, her critical voice would pounce, mocking her dreams as a waste of time and reminding her of her lack of talent. Her critical voice kept her from even opening to, much less believing in, the possibility that she could be a successful photographer. I knew that I needed to ally myself with the part that was struggling to emerge. One day she asked if I wanted to see some of her work. Seeing it, I immediately understood why she had received so much encouragement. Unfortunately, her magnificent talent was buried under a barrage of self-criticism and self-doubt.

A dream early in our work highlighted her fears of revealing herself to me and to herself. In the dream, Claudia was in a crowded restaurant eating breakfast alone. Suddenly a piece of bagel got lodged in her throat. She couldn't use her voice to cry for help, and she knew that if she didn't "get it out," she would die. As we worked with the dream, Claudia confided to me that she was afraid I would see her as weak and needy. I told her that I sensed that she was hurting and afraid of hurting even more and that it was very scary to have me know this, even though a part of her really wanted me to know. My expression of her ambivalent attitude at first relieved her but then, not surprisingly, scared her. Although she wanted me to know her, she was certain that if I really did, I would find her damaged and unlovable core and leave. I sensed that her projection about me reflected an internal conflict within herself. Indeed, that proved to be true. Claudia was afraid that whatever she found out about herself would be too much to bear—so bad that, in fact, she feared it would kill her. But to abandon the search meant a continuation of her misery. Of course I didn't know this at the time, but as the therapy progressed, it became clearer that the stakes were that high and Claudia's conflict tied her in knots. Time and again, when Claudia felt seen by me, she would clam up. Her silence was her attempt to wall off her inner self—not only from me but more importantly from herself. I knew I had to go very slow and respect her protective patterns.

Claudia revealed another dream one day. In it she asks me if she can come twice a week, and I say no. She tells me that I say no because I believe that nothing is really wrong with her. The dream revealed Claudia's inner confusion as to whether she's really okay and only creating problems or whether there really is something wrong. Again she externalized it onto me. In the dream I confirm one side of her fear—that she is making "mountains out of molehills." The other side of her fear is that she is so damaged, there is no hope. I recognized this as she shared the dream and consequently responded carefully:

"In your dream I think that there's nothing really wrong with you. Do you want to ask me what I really think?"

Claudia looked fearful, but determined, and said, "Yes, I do. Do you think there's something wrong with me?"

"Let me put it this way. I see your fear and sense your hurt and pain even though it seems you don't know much about it yet. I don't think you're making anything up. I think you're wanting to come more often because you're feeling scared about something—perhaps you know what you're scared about and can't tell me yet or perhaps you just feel fear and don't know much more than that. Whatever it is, I think coming more often is a good idea. Hopefully getting together twice a week will help you feel safer and less scared."

Claudia smiled and let out her breath. "Thank you. I'm glad you're okay with meeting more often, but now that I've asked, I'm scared of what I've gotten myself into."

We began meeting twice a week and about 6 months later increased our meetings to three times a week. This began after Claudia started having disturbing nightmares and memories of her father sexually abusing her when she was little. Claudia's memories were triggered after she was given anesthesia for a tooth extraction.

Her nightmares and memories terrified and disturbed her, so much so that Claudia couldn't share them with me. Even so, I could see that she was upset and trapped in her silence. She tried to tell me by canceling appointments, saying "I just can't do this today." Being of the mind that a client has that choice, I at first didn't call her back. This, I soon learned, was a mistake. When she didn't receive a call, she assumed either that I didn't care about her or that she was fine.

After several reoccurrences of this pattern and some discussion with her, I finally understood that Claudia needed me to reach out to her at these times, even if she insisted she was "fine" because she was too trapped behind her wall of fear and shame to reach out to me. I wish I had been able to understand what Claudia needed sooner. I'm afraid that early in our work I failed Claudia all too often. It was a combination of her determination to keep me at arms length and my difficulty in appreciating her inability to cope with the material emerging in her nightmares and memories. I guess I was sufficiently empathic with Claudia during this time; she gave me many chances to learn what she needed. As I did, her trust in me grew.

Our work continued for several years in this way, some disclosure and trust building, then silence. We seemed to be in a holding pattern. I continued to ally myself with the side of Claudia that wanted to emerge, patiently holding steady when the other side slapped her down or terrified her. Because she couldn't speak about her memories and dreams, she coped with her terror and pain by cutting her legs. One day she admitted to cutting; she said it had scared her so much that she wouldn't do it again. But she did do it again and then again. She seemed to feel at this point that she had crossed a line, which meant she no longer could tell me about it. When finally I guessed, she was visibly relieved that I saw through her wall of silence. After some wrangling she agreed to call me if she felt the urge to do it again. I suggested that she continue to come more frequently and told her not to hesitate to call if she felt in trouble. I began reaching out to her in between sessions just to let her know I was there for her. Sometimes she would call, asking to come in for another session but once there, she would be unable to speak. She would try but then would stop, locked in silence, staring out the window.

Working with Claudia was extremely difficult for me during this phase. I am grateful that my consultation group was able to give me support and helpful feedback because Claudia's silence made it difficult for me to gauge the level of her despair. I feared she might hurt herself or worse. Several times when things got critical, I shared my fears and sense of helplessness with her. Twice I insisted that if she didn't tell me what was going on, I would have no choice but to hospitalize her. Setting those limits both relieved and contained her. She always responded by letting me know what her pain was about. It wasn't just Claudia's silence that often created difficulty for me. Her negative transferences (projecting on to me her angry and intrusive father and/or her oblivious mother) sometimes challenged me to remain steady. Often suspicious and vigilant, she scrutinized every gesture and inflection of mine for signs of rejection, judgment, or betrayal. At those times I felt under a microscope, sometimes frustrated by her inability to encounter *me* and not her ghosts. I knew that what she needed most was my steadiness because that would help her see me, trust in me, and feel secure in knowing that I would not desert her under any circumstances. My stance, sometimes verbalized, sometimes implied, was: "I'm here, I care about you, and we will get through this together. Your silence and vigilance exists to protect you. It isn't going to push me away or make me mad. It's safe to open the door and let me in."

At times she was able to tell me about her memories and nightmares. Most would involve her father, coming up to her room when she was a little girl and hurting her either sexually, physically, or emotionally. She struggled to express the nightmares and memories, asking me occasionally to sit next to her, which I did. I tried to help her separate from the memories using the modified EMDR technique (Shapiro, 1998; see chap. 4 of this volume). I suggested that she view her memories as if she were on a train and they were like the scenery passing by. I said things like, "Watch them go by as if watching the scenery on a train, Claudia. You're safe here with me." Sometimes this helped her stay present, but so often she couldn't and disconnected from her memories and me. All I could do then was remind her of where she was, hoping that she could hear me. These sessions would often be followed again by silence. She feared disclosing the nightmares, which then confirmed a damaged self to me and to herself. She knew she was caught in a dilemma. She was afraid to trust and tried to keep me out, but when she did, she got scared because the "it doesn't matter" voice, which was in place to protect her from the pain, was reckless: When it was in charge, she cut herself.

Claudia's battle, personality characteristics, and protective mechanisms were similar to many adults who suffered sexual and emotional abuse as a child. I believe that existential therapy, with its emphasis on personal and relational presence, provides survivors of sexual abuse with an extremely effective healing milieu. Fisher (2005) effectively elaborates on this perspective. Like Claudia, adult survivors of sexual abuse feel damaged, disconnected from themselves, and mistrustful of others. As Claudia opened up to herself and to me for the first time, the early trauma was reactivated.

Claudia faced several challenges at the same time. First, she was challenged to incorporate a heretofore subconscious aspect of herself as an incest survivor into her sense of self. It directly countered her "I am tough and strong, you can't hurt me" persona. Second, she had to acknowledge not only her father's anger toward her but now his outright abuse of her. Third, she was challenged to trust me. Although she wanted my help, she struggled with letting me get close. She feared that if she revealed herself to me, I would leave like everyone else. Finally, she felt so damaged that she couldn't believe that a better life was possible for her. Death was a back door that ironically allowed her to live another day. She knew how dangerous this thinking was but held on to it for a long time. When she finally let it go some 3 years later, she had, to some extent, incorporated her four challenges to accept her identity as an incest survivor, to accept her father's abuse, to trust me more, and to believe in the possibility of a better life. Even more important was the fact that in choosing life, she had closed the door on death as a way out of her misery. This marked the end of Phase One of our therapy. What follows is a condensed version of the events in this pivotal period.

Claudia told me about her decision to live after the fact, when we resumed our work following a 2-week Christmas break. She told me she had fully intended to kill herself over the break. A job as photojournalist with a travel magazine fell through, and her attempts to develop her photography business was proving difficult. She felt unable to get any "traction" in her life despite all her efforts, and on top of it all, she was still alone. She was devastated. She believed that nothing would change. But something did change for her when she actually faced death. She realized she could do it, that she *could choose* to die, and with that realization, she chose instead to live. In that moment she began to accept her identity as a survivor and all of life's challenges.

One particular question that challenged Claudia soon after the aforementioned incident was, "Who am I going to be now?" Claudia's question highlights the functionality and tenacity of our self and world constructs. Although they limit us, they also serve to shape our sense of identity. We typically feel notably shaky when we choose to shed some of the old constructs and create new ones. This was my challenge in Phase Two—to help Claudia forge a new sense of self that acknowledged the past but held hope for the future. Our therapy was radically different in this phase. With our therapeutic relationship stronger, Claudia felt safer in it and more trusting of me. In Phase Two a client's anxiety is often replaced by willingness. This was true for Claudia, although she still experienced significant anxiety. But because she trusted me more, she was able to express her feelings more easily. When she got scared and put up a wall, she could speak from her fears and mistrust instead of acting them out. For the most part, she experienced me as her ally and not her enemy, and when she did see me as the enemy, we worked through it. She was challenged in this phase to incorporate her sense of herself as an incest survivor, to face her hurt and anger toward her parents, to begin to love herself, and to experience herself as lovable, talented, and competent. Our work focused on the ways in which she blocked herself from these aspects of herself—her belief in her damaged self, her fear of failure, her mistrust of others, and her cruel, harsh, and demanding voice that often ran the show.

This phase lasted several years in which she worked very hard to accept her past, to be present in the moment, and to develop a future. We worked with many dreams and memories. She struggled to experience her feelings and to express them in the moment. When she disengaged from her feelings, talking in the third person, I encouraged her to make I-statements. She still edited her thoughts before speaking and often struggled not to feel something if she didn't know what it meant. I tried to help her accept her feelings and to express her wants and wishes.

She decided at some point to tell her mother and her siblings about the sexual abuse. None of them believed her, with the exception of one brother. She had hoped her mother and brothers would embrace her, but instead they either denied it or, in the case of one brother, told her to just put it in the past. It was a very painful time, full of anger, self-doubt, and despair. But she weathered it bravely. She continued to paint and take photographs, which gave her a constructive outlet for her pain. At the same time she decided to enroll in an art therapy program to learn how to use such therapy with sexually abused children. By the end of this phase, Claudia was experiencing herself as much more than "a damaged loser." Her photography business was taking off and she was working as an art therapist with children at a local hospital. She met and began to date "Garth," a very good man whom she liked and trusted.

The end of this phase was marked by a pivotal session, abbreviated here:

Claudia comes in, looking drawn, and says, "I just want to take a break." Tears stream down her face, and she struggles to hold them back.

I mirror back her struggle not to feel, and she says, "I just don't know what it means. There's no reason for me to feel this way." She then begins to list all the good things that are happening to her.

I say, "When you shut the door on your feelings like you just did, you lose the chance to find out what's going on. Are you willing to leave the door open for a bit?"

She agrees and I suggest that she let herself freely associate to the phrase, "I just want to take a break," trying not to edit, just letting whatever is there to be spoken.

"Okay," she says, and then slowly, being present to herself, she begins, "I just want to take a break from my work. I just want to take a break from my painting. I just want to take a break from my family." With those words, her tears start freshly flowing.

Through her tears she says, "I'm tired of thinking about them. I'm tired of wishing they would change." She pauses and then in a stronger voice says, "I'm tired of thinking about myself only in that way" (being abused by her father).

Claudia stops, and then looks at me, "I don't mean that I want to dismiss it."

"I didn't hear that," I say. "I think you're saying that you know that it's a part of who you are but not all of you."

She nods and says, "That's it." She continues, "I never thought I'd be saying that or feeling that. It's been such a long time—I *am* more than what happened to me."

The final phase of therapy, or Phase Three, is typically marked by a great deal of creativity. This was certainly true in Claudia's case. Within a number of years Claudia was able to create a life of purpose, meaning, and intimate relationships. She is still with Garth and has developed many other intimate relationships. She has a successful photography business and has continued to work with abused children, deriving great satisfaction from this volunteer work.

But life has by no means been rosy for Claudia. She lost a close friend during this time and faced and worked through significant fears triggered by her increasingly intimate relationship with Garth. Not surprisingly, even though she loved Garth, she occasionally projected her father onto him. At those times she experienced him as angry, scary, and uncaring. Then she reacted as a terrified little girl or as a rebellious teenager, impervious to pain. Both stances protected her from her core fear and feeling that Garth and everyone else would eventually go away because she was damaged and unlovable.

It is so important to appreciate the tenacity of negative core beliefs. They do not resolve easily. Resolution occurs through a reiterative process that provides the client with multiple opportunities: first to be open to their locked-away feelings and then to have a corrective experience of them. Claudia and I became quite familiar with this reiterative process. But working with her core issues in Phase Three was quite different. Unlike earlier in therapy, now Claudia recognized what was happening. She wasn't as caught in it as before. She could step back and experience coming from "her little girl" place or coming from her "her rebellious teenager" place. She recognized them now as two patterns of being, each trying to protect her from the pain of being unlovable.

A brief exchange between me and Claudia illustrates this point.

Late in a session, Claudia assumes her "her rebellious teenager" stance, unwilling to talk further about a recent exchange with Garth—sure in that moment that Garth wouldn't take her needs into consideration and would eventually leave like everyone else.

"The 13-year-old seems to be running the show right now," I say.

"It's easier to feel hate than feel pain," Claudia responds. "My 2-year-old trusted my father and then he turned on me."

I ask, "Can you try and let yourself open to what you're experiencing right now instead of having the 13-year-old shut you down?"

She takes several deep breaths, and slowly her expression changes from anger to sadness. She turns and looks at me with tears in her eyes.

"I'm afraid to open to Garth. I'm afraid I'm too much to love."

Her eyes fill with tears, and she turns away from me. She seems to be disconnecting from me and her painful feelings of being "too much to love." I mirror that back to her and suggest that she make eye contact with me. She tries and then looks away again.

"When I look at you, I feel like something bad will happen." She tries to maintain eye contact with me as she tells me this but can't and looks away again.

"And now you go away again," I say softly and gently. I am silent and wait, silently calling her back to be with me in our room. "Where are you now?"

Looking at me she says, "I move away and I watch." I smile at her, but she quickly looks away. She falls silent again, but soon I notice something has changed on Claudia's face. Her sadness has been replaced by a smile. I note her smile and ask, "What's happening now?"

"I'm sitting on a curb—I'm little and you're sitting right next to me. I don't have to do anything." Looking at me, she says, "You're okay with me."

"Yes, I am, Claudia, very okay with you." Our eyes, full of tears, meet, and we grin at each other—no need for words now.

In this significant session Claudia and I revisited her fear of being too much to love. First she went to the fearful, then sad place. But by allowing herself to be present with me and not transfer "dad" experiences onto me, she could experience me as I was: safe, trustworthy, and caring. With a shift in her experience of me, she was able to experience herself in a more accepting and loving way.

Slowly over many years, Claudia shed her sense of self as damaged, incompetent, and unlovable. Those feelings were replaced with feelings of acceptability, lovability, and capability. At the end of our therapy she told me that what helped her most was knowing that I always believed in her. She was right—I always did.

Glossary of Key Terms

AWE   The humility and wonder, "bigger picture" of living, often attained by clients following the removal of blocks to their innermost sensibilities about life, their maximal ranges of experience. The sense of awe is an increasingly recognized spiritual dimension of intensive E–H practice, and a vital context for the optimal appreciation of life.

CLIENT'S BATTLE   Refers to the client's internal struggle between the part that endeavors to emerge and the part that endeavors to resist, or block the emerging.

COMMITMENT   Refers to a sense of "I-ness" or agency, or profound caring about a given direction. It implies assumption of personal responsibility and a sense that the life one chooses really matters to oneself and is worth a full investment.

CONFRONTATION   An amplified form of vivification of resistance; instead of alerting clients to their self-destructive patterns, it alarms them and presses for transformation.

CONSTRICTIVE/EXPANSIVE CONTINUUM   Kirk Schneider's understanding of personality functioning as a range within which humans have a vast capacity to "draw back" and constrict thoughts, feelings, and sensations, as well as an equivalent capacity to "burst forth" and expand thoughts, feelings, and sensations.

CULTIVATING PRESENCE   A therapeutic method and goal characterized by openness, engagement, and deep attunement to the unfolding processes of both client and therapist, with the intention of illuminating the client's self and world constructs in the therapeutic encounter.

CULTIVATING AWE   A therapeutic goal characterized by clients' renewed abilities to experience the fullness of their lives—their deepest dreads as well as most dazzling desires—and their rejuvenated capacity for choice.

EMBODIED MEDITATION   Concerted attention to body sensations, often accompanied by invitations to the client to place her or his hand on areas noted, such as tension areas or areas that feel blocked. Initial invitations are often followed by further invitations to associate feelings, sensations, or images to the aforementioned areas.

EXPERIENTIAL MODALITY   Embraces four basic dimensions—the immediate, the kinesthetic, the affective, and the profound or cosmic. The road to an expanded identity is to help clients experience their polarized conditions, assist them to "embody" those conditions, and to attune to the nature of those conditions.

EXISTENCE   The central focus of existential therapy, whose Latin root *ex* ("out from") and *sistere* ("to stand") means "to stand out from" or "become."

EXISTENTIAL–HUMANISTIC (E–H) THERAPY   Form of therapy that emphasizes freedom, experiential (or whole-bodied) reflection, and responsibility (or the ability to respond to one's freedom and reflection); E–H therapy, as described in this volume, refers broadly to the U.S. version of existential therapy, which overlaps with other humanistically oriented therapies but with an accent on struggle, circumspection, and depth.

EXISTENTIAL–INTEGRATIVE (EI) THERAPY   Mode of therapy inspired by May and Bugental and developed by Schneider that coordinates a variety of therapeutic modalities within an overarching existential or experiential context.

EXISTENTIAL PREDICAMENT   A major focus of existential psychotherapy that refers to the fact that every person is aware of his or her existence and consequently must cope in various ways with this awareness.

EXISTENTIAL STANCES   The conditions through which experiential liberation and transformation can take place. E–H stances (intertwining and overlapping) include the cultivation of presence (presence as ground); the cultivation and activation of therapeutic presence through struggle (presence as a method and goal); the encounter with resistance to the therapeutic struggle; and the coalescence of the meaning, intentionality, and life-awakening (awe) that can result from the struggle.

FREEDOM AND DESTINY   Refers to the capacity for choice (freedom) within the natural and self-imposed limits (destiny) of living. The challenge to respond to these polarities is central to leading E–H theorists' conception of psychological health.

GIVENS OF HUMAN EXISTENCE   Yalom conceives of four "givens": death, freedom, isolation, and meaninglessness; the design and quality of our lives depends on how we confront these givens. Greening understands these four givens as paradoxical dialectics that present us with life challenges.

HUMAN-BEING-IN-THE-WORLD   E–H practitioners understand a person as related to her or his physical, personal, and social worlds; sense of self or identity is formed as a result of this interrelation of person and world.

"I AM" EXPERIENCE   Rollo May's phrase describing the experience of identity formation, which includes the fact of awareness and the drive to make meaning of it through an ongoing dialectical process between the subjective and objective poles of reality.

INTERPERSONAL PRESENCE   Refers to the capacity to be present to experiences, feelings, and attitudes occurring between therapist and client that are implicitly or explicitly unfolding in the present moment in the therapy room; the terms *interpersonal processes* and *intersubjective processes* are also frequently used in this regard.

INTRAPERSONAL PRESENCE   Refers to the capacity to be present to inner experiences, memories, feelings, and attitudes that are implicitly and explicitly unfolding in the present moment in the therapy room; the terms *intrapsychic* and *subjective* also connote the intrapersonal realm.

INVOKING THE ACTUAL   Helping the client into that which is palpably relevant or charged to call attention to the part of the client that is attempting to emerge or to a resistance or protection that is blocking emergence.

LIFE MEANING   Occurs as clients face and overcome blocks to their aliveness and begin to choose their paths and assert themselves; the working through of resistance or protective patterns is preparatory to the unfolding of meaning.

NOTING   An aspect of vivifying resistance that apprises the client of initial experiences of resistance.

OCTAVES FOR ACTIVATING PRESENCE   James Bugental's strategies of activating clients' presence, which include listening, guiding, instructing, and requiring.

PASSION FOR FORM   Rollo May's phrase for each person's dialectical process of meaning making, which May believed to be the essence of genuine creativity.

PHENOMENOLOGICAL PHILOSOPHY   The basic philosophy of the phenomological mehod, which is the chief empirical base for existential theory and therapy. The phenomenological method emphasizes intimate and detailed description of lived experience.

PRESENCE   A foundational element of existential therapy, whose Latin root is *prae* ("before") and *esse* (to be), meaning "to be before." Presence is the capacity to be before or to be with one's being and/or to be before or to be with another human being. Presence assumes both availability and expressiveness. It holds and illuminates that which is palpably (immediately, affectively, kinesthetically, and profoundly) relevant within the client and between client and therapist.

PROCESS VS. CONTENT   Refers to the therapist's attention to the pre-verbal/kinesthetic way the client talks more than what the client says. Attention to the way clients hold themselves, their vocal fluctuations and breathing, and the way they relate to the therapist.

RESISTANCE OR PROTECTION   The blockage to that which is palpably (immediately, affectively, kinesthetically) relevant within the client and between client and therapist. E–H practitioners assume that resistances or protections are concrete manifestations of some aspect of a client's self and world construct system.

RESPONSIBILITY ASSUMPTION   Acceptance by the client of responsibility for creating her or his life situation, thus enabling her or him to choose differently in the future; a critical goal for E–H therapists.

REVISITATION   A key therapeutic dimension in which clients cycle through the ways in which they stop or block themselves from fuller personal and interpersonal presence; also called *reiteration*. Many revisitations are typically required before "stuck" ways of being can be accessed. Each time a revisitation occurs, clients learn more about their willingness to approach such situations in the future.

REVITALIZATION OR INTENTIONALITY   The full-bodied orientation to a given goal or direction; differs from intellectual or behavioral change in that its impetus derives from the client's entire sense of being, import, and priority.

SELF AND WORLD CONSTRUCTS   Refers to the client's construal of existence, both conscious and subconscious, as derived from the client's unique shaping of his or her subjective experiences with the objective world. A person's self and world constructs are present in the living moment but may be hidden from consciousness.

TAGGING   *Alerts* clients to the repetition of their resistance; implies a subtle challenge to reassess their ways of being and take responsibility for their self-constructions.

THERAPEUTIC ENCOUNTER   Refers to a caring meeting between two human beings in which the therapist consciously cultivates a collaborative relationship. The E–H encounter assumes that how the client relates to the therapist is how she or he relates to others. The encounter can mean calling attention to undercurrents in the immediate and evolving relationship, the recognition of transference and countertransference projections, or the exploration of the therapeutic bond.

TRACING OUT   Another form of vivifying resistance that encourages clients to explore the fantasized consequences of their resistance—for example, the fantasized consequences of weight loss.

TRANSFERENCE   An aspect of the therapeutic encounter that refers to a client's protective, patterned ways of being with self and other that is reactivated in the therapeutic relationship. Working through the negative transference in the here and now allows the client to shed constricted ways of being.

VIVIFICATION OF RESISTANCE   The intensification (or mirroring) of clients' awareness of how they block or limit themselves; vivification alerts clients to these blocks or limits, while confrontation alarms them.

WORKING IN THE HERE AND NOW   The E–H emphasis on the intra- and interpersonal processes that are implicitly and explicitly unfolding in the present moment in the therapy room.

WORKING SPACE   The pause that helps the therapist to understand and, more importantly, to assist the client to vivify (or intensely elucidate) herself or himself.

Suggested Readings/ Web Resources

Becker, E. (1973). *Denial of death.* New York: Free Press.

Bugental, J. F. T. (1976). *The search for existential identity.* San Francisco: Jossey-Bass.

Bugental, J. F. T. (1999). *Psychotherapy isn't what you think.* Phoenix, AZ: Zeig, Tucker.

Cain, D. J., & Seeman, J. (Eds.). (2002). *Humanistic psychotherapies: Handbook of research and practice.* Washington, DC: American Psychological Association.

Cooper, M. (2003). *Existential therapies.* London: Sage.

Laing, R. D. (1969). *The divided self: An existential study in sanity and madness.* Middlesex, UK: Penguin.

May, R., Angel, E., & Ellenberger, H. (Eds.). (1958). *Existence: A new dimension inpsychiatry and psychology.* New York: Basic Books.

Mendelowitz, E., & Schneider, K. (2008). Existential psychotherapy. In R. Corsini & D. Wedding (Eds.), *Current psychotherapies* (8th ed., pp. 295–326). Belmont, CA: Thompson/Brooks Cole.

Schneider, K. J. (Ed.). (2008). *Existential–integrative psychotherapy: Guideposts to the core of practice.* New York: Routledge.

Schneider, K. J., Bugental, J. F. T., & Pierson, J. F. (Eds.). (2001). *The handbook of humanistic psychology: Leading edges in theory, research, and practice.* Thousand Oaks, CA: Sage.

Schneider, K. J., & May, R. (1995). *The psychology of existence: An integrative, clinical perspective.* New York: McGraw-Hill.

Yalom, I. (1980). *Existential psychotherapy.* New York: Basic Books.

Yalom, I. (2002). *The gift of therapy.* New York: HarperCollins.

WEB RESOURCES

Bugental, J. F. T. (Speaker). (2005). *Existential-humanistic psychotherapy in action* [DVD]. San Francisco: Psychotherapy.net

Existential-Humanistic Institute. (n.d.). Existential-Humanistic Institute Web page. Retrieved April 5, 2009, from http://www.ehinstitute.org

Hoffman, L. (2005). *Why become an existential therapist?* Retrieved April 5, 2009, from the Depth Psychotherapy Network Web site: http://www.depth-psychotherapy-network.com/Student_Section/Orientation_Overviews/Existential_Psychotherapy/Existential_Psychotherapy_Students.htm

May, R. (Speaker). (2007). *Rollo May on existential psychotherapy* [DVD]. San Francisco: Psychotherapy.net

Schneider, K. J. (Speaker). (2006). *Existential therapy* [DVD and online article]. Washington, DC: American Psychological Association. Retrieved June 11, 2009, from http://www.apa.org/videos/4310756.html.

Schneider, K. J. (Speaker). (2009). *Existential–Humanistic Therapy Over Time.* [DVD set and online article]. Washington, DC: American Psychological Association. Retrieved June 11, 2009, from http://www.apa.org/videos/4310567.html.

Yalom, I. (Speaker). (2005). *Irvin Yalom: Live case consultation* [DVD]. San Francisco: Psychotherapy.net

References

Alsup, R. (2008). Existentialism of personalism: A Native American perspective. In K. J. Schneider (Ed.), *Existential–integrative psychotherapy: Guideposts to the core of practice* (pp. 121–127). New York: Routledge.

APA Task Force on Evidence–Based Practice. (2006). Evidence-based practice in psychology. *American Psychologist, 61*, 271–285.

Assisting youth with understanding the impact of civility and violence within their communities. (2007, June). *Ernest Becker Foundation Newsletter, 14*, 3.

Ballinger, B., Matano, R., & Amantea, A. (2008). A perspective on alcoholism: The case of Charles. In K. J. Schneider (Ed.), *Existential–integrative psychotherapy: Guideposts to the core of practice* (pp. 177–185). New York: Routledge.

Barrett, W. H. (1958). *Irrational man: A study in existential philosophy.* New York: Doubleday.

Becker, E. (1973). *Denial of death.* New York: Free Press.

Binswanger, L. (1958). The case of Ellen West. In R. May, E. Angel, & H. Ellenberger (Eds.), *Existence* (pp. 237–364). New York: Basic Books.

Bohart, A. C., & Greenberg, L. S. (Eds). (1997). *Empathy reconsidered.* Washington, DC: American Psychological Association.

Bohart, A. C., O'Hara, M., & Leitner, L. M. (1998). Empirically violated treatments: Disenfranchisement of humanistic and other psychotherapies. *Psychotherapy Research, 8*, 141–157.

Bohart, A. C., O'Hara, M., Leitner, L. M., Wertz, F. J., Stern, E. M., Schneider, K. J., et al. (1997). Guidelines for the provision of humanistic psychosocial services. *Humanistic Psychologist, 24*, 64–107.

Bohart, A. C., & Tallman, K. (1999). *How clients make therapy work: The process of active self-healing.* Washington, DC: American Psychological Association.

Boss, M. (1963). *Psychoanalysis and daseinanalysis.* New York: Basic Books.

Bowman, P. (1995). An existential–spiritual perspective: The case of Sarah. In K. J. Schneider and R. May (Eds.), *The psychology of existence: An integrative, clinical perspective* (pp. 293–301). New York: McGraw-Hill.

Bradford, G. K. (2007). The play of unconditioned presence in existential–integrative psychotherapy. *Journal of Transpersonal Psychology, 39,* 23–47.

Brown, L. S. (2008). Feminist therapy as meaning-making practice: Where there is no power, where is the meaning? In K. J. Schneider (Ed.), *Existential–integrative psychotherapy: Guideposts to the core of practice* (pp. 130–140). New York: Routledge.

Buber, M. (1970). *I and thou* (W. Kaufmann, Trans.). New York: Scribner's. (Original work published 1937)

Bugental, E. (2008). Swimming together in a sea of loss: A group process for elders. In K. J. Schneider (Ed.), *Existential–integrative psychotherapy: Guideposts to the core of practice* (pp. 333–342). New York: Routledge.

Bugental, J. F. T. (1965). *The search for authenticity: An existential–analytic approach to psychotherapy.* New York: Holt, Rinehart, & Winston.

Bugental, J. F. T. (1976). *The search for existential identity: Patient-therapist dialogues in humanistic psychotherapy.* San Francisco: Jossey-Bass.

Bugental, J. F. T. (1978). *Psychotherapy and process: The fundamentals of an existential–humanistic approach.* New York: McGraw-Hill.

Bugental, J. F. T. (1987). *The art of the psychotherapist.* New York: Norton.

Bugental, J. F. T. (1999). *Psychotherapy isn't what you think.* Phoenix, AZ: Zeig, Tucker.

Bugental, J. F. T. (2008). Preliminary sketches for a short-term existential therapy. In K. J. Schneider (Ed.), *Existential–integrative psychotherapy: Guideposts to the core of practice* (pp. 165–168). New York: Routledge.

Bugental, J. F. T., & Bracke, P. (1992). The future of existential–humanistic psychotherapy. *Psychotherapy, 29,* 28–33.

Bugental, J. F. T., & Kleiner, R. (1993). Existential psychotherapies. In G. Stricker & G. Gold (Eds.), *Comprehensive handbook of psychotherapy integration.* New York: Plenum.

Bugental, J. F. T., & Sterling, M. (1995). Existential psychotherapy. In A. S. Gurman & S. B. Messer (Eds.), *Essential psychotherapies* (pp. 226–260). New York: Guilford Press.

Bunting, K., & Hayes, S. (2008). Language and meaning: Acceptance and commitment therapy and the EI model. In K. J. Schneider (Ed.), *Existential–integrative psychotherapy: Guideposts to the core of practice* (pp. 217–234). New York: Routledge.

Burston, D. (2003). Existentialism, humanism, and psychotherapy. *Existential Analysis, 14,* 309–319.

Cain, D. J., & Seeman, J. (Eds.). (2002). *Humanistic psychotherapies: Handbook of research and practice.* Washington, DC: American Psychological Association.

Calton, T., Ferriter, M., Huband, N., & Spandler, H. (2008). A systematic review of the Soteria paradigm for the treatment of people diagnosed with schizophrenia. *Schizophrenia Bulletin, 34,* 181–192.

Camus, A. (1955). *The myth of Sisyphus and other essays* (J. O'Brien, Trans.). New York: Knopf.

Churchill, S., & Wertz, F. J. (2001). An introduction to phenomenological research in psychology: Historical, conceptual, and methodological foundations. In K. J. Schneider, J. F. T. Bugental, & J. F. Pierson (Eds.), *The handbook of humanistic psychology: Leading edges in theory, practice, and research* (pp. 247–262). Thousand Oaks, CA: Sage.

Comas-Diaz, L. (2008). Latino psychospirituality. In K. J. Schneider (Ed.), *Existential–integrative psychotherapy: Guideposts to the core of practice* (pp. 100–109). New York: Routledge.

Cooper, M. (2003). *Existential therapies.* London: Sage.

Cooper, M. (2004). Viagra for the brain: Psychotherapy research and the challenge to existential therapeutic practice. *Existential Analysis, 15,* 2–14.

Cooper, M. (2008). Interpersonal perceptions and metaperceptions: Psychotherapeutic practice in the interexperiential realm. *Journal of Humanistic Psychology, 49*(1), 85–99.

Cortright, B. (1997). *Psychotherapy and spirit: Theory and practice in transpersonal psychotherapy.* New York: SUNY Press.

Craig, P. E. (1986). Sanctuary and presence: An existential view of the therapist's contribution. *The Humanistic Psychologist, 14*(1), 22–28.

Criswell, E. (2001). Humanistic psychology and mind/body medicine. In K. J. Schneider, J. F. T. Bugental, & J. F. Pierson (Eds.), *The handbook of humanistic psychology: Leading edges in theory, practice, and research* (pp. 581–591). Thousand Oaks, CA: Sage.

Cushman, P. (1995). *Constructing the self, constructing America: A cultural history of psychotherapy.* Reading, MA: Addison-Wesley.

deBeauvoir, S. (1948). *The ethics of ambiguity.* New York: Citadel.

de Quincey, C. (2002). *Radical nature: Rediscovering the soul of matter.* Montpelier, VT: Invisible Cities Press.

DeCarvalho, R. (1991). *The founders of humanistic psychology.* New York: Praeger.

Decker, L. (2007). Combat trauma: Treatment from a mystical/spiritual perspective. *Journal of Humanistic Psychology, 47,* 30–53.

Dorman, D. (2008). Dante's cure: Schizophrenia and the two-person journey. In K. J. Schneider (Ed.), *Existential–integrative psychotherapy: Guideposts to the core of practice* (pp. 236–245). New York: Routledge.

Elkins, D. (2007). Empirically supported treatments: The deconstruction of a myth. *Journal of Humanistic Psychology, 47,* 474–500.

Elkins, D. N. (2001). Beyond religion: Toward a humanistic spirituality. In K. J. Schneider, J. F. T. Bugental, & J. F. Pierson (Eds.), *The handbook of humanistic psychology: Leading edges in theory, practice, and research* (pp. 201–212). Thousand Oaks, CA: Sage.

Elliott, R. (2002). The effectiveness of humanistic therapies: A meta-analysis. In D. J. Cain & J. Seeman (Eds.), *Humanistic psychotherapies: Handbook of research and practice* (pp. 57–81). Washington, DC: American Psychological Association.

Elliott, R., & Greenberg, L. S. (2002). Process-experiential psychotherapy. In D. J. Cain & J. Seeman (Eds.), *Humanistic psychotherapies: Handbook of research and practice* (pp. 279–306). Washington, DC: American Psychological Association.

Fauth, J., Gates, S., Vinca, M. A., & Boles, S. (2007). Big ideas for psychotherapy training. *Psychotherapy: Theory, Research, Practice, Training, 44,* 384–391.

Fischer, C. T. (1994). *Individualizing psychological assessment.* Hillsdale, NJ: Erlbaum.

Fisher, G. (2005). Existential psychotherapy with adult survivors of sexual abuse. *Journal of Humanistic Psychology, 45,* 10–40.

Flach, F. (1990). Disorders of the pathways involved in the creative process. In A. Runco & R. Richards (Eds.), *Eminent creativity, everyday creativity, and health* (pp. 179–189). Westport, CT: Ablex/Greenwood.

Fosha, D. (2008). Transformance, recognition of self by self, and effective action. In K. J. Schneider (Ed.), *Existential–integrative psychotherapy: Guideposts to the core of practice* (pp. 290–320). New York: Routledge.

Frankl, V. E. (1963). *Man's search for meaning: An introduction to logotherapy.* New York: Pocket Books.

Friedman, M. (1991a). *The worlds of existentialism: A critical reader.* Atlantic Highlands, NJ: Humanities Press.

Friedman, M. (1991b). *Encounter on the narrow ridge: A life of Martin Buber.* New York: Paragon House.

Friedman, M. (1995). The case of Dawn. In K. J. Schneider & R. May (Eds.), *The psychology of existence: An integrative, clinical perspective* (pp. 308–315). New York: McGraw-Hill.

Friedman, M. (2001). Expanding the boundaries of theory. In K. J. Schneider, J. F. T. Bugental, & J. F. Pierson (Eds.), *The handbook of humanistic psychology: Leading edges in theory, practice, and research* (pp. 343–348). Thousand Oaks, CA: Sage.

Fromm, E. (1941). *Escape from freedom.* New York: Holt, Rinehart, & Winston.

Galvin, J. (2008). Brief encounters with Chinese clients: The case of Peter. In K. J. Schneider (Ed.), *Existential–integrative psychotherapy: Guideposts to the core of practice* (pp. 168–175). New York: Routledge.

Gendlin, E. T. (1996). *Focusing-oriented psychotherapy.* New York: Guilford.

Giorgi, A. (1970). *Psychology as a human science: A phenomenologically based approach.* New York: Harper & Row.

Goldfried, M. R., & Wolfe, B. E. (1996). Psychotherapy practice and research: Repairing a strained alliance. *American Psychologist, 51,* 1007–1016.

Greenberg, L. S. (2007). Emotion coming of age. *Clinical Psychology: Science and Practice, 14,* 414–421.

Greenberg, L. S., Rice, L. N., & Elliott, R. (1993). *Facilitating emotional change: The moment-by-moment process.* New York: Guilford Press.

Greening. T. (1992). Existential challenges and responses. *The Humanistic Psychologist, 20*(1), 111–115.

Grondin, J. (1995). *Sources of hermeneutics.* Albany: State University of New York Press.

Gurman, A. S., & Messer, S. B. (Eds.). (2003). *Essential psychotherapies* (2nd ed.). New York: Guilford Press.

Hanna, F. J., Giordano, F., Dupuy, P., & Puhakka, K. (1995). Agency and transcendence: The experience of therapeutic change. *Humanistic Psychologist, 23,* 139–160.

Heidegger, M. (1962). *Being and time* (J. Macquarrie & E. Robinson, Trans.). New York: Basic Books.

Hillman, J., & Ventura, M. (1992). *We've had a hundred years of psychotherapy and the world's getting worse.* San Francisco: HarperSanFrancisco.

Hoffman, L. (2008). An EI approach to working with religious and spiritual clients. In K. J. Schneider (Ed.), *Existential–integrative psychotherapy: Guideposts to the core of practice* (pp. 187–201). New York: Routledge.

Hoffman, L., Stewart, S., Warren, W., & Meek, L. (2009). Toward a sustainable myth of self: An existential response to the postmodern condition. *Journal of Humanistic Psychology, 49,* 135–173.

Hoffman, L., Yang, M., Kaklauskas, F., & Chan, A. (2009). *Existential psychology East-West.* Colorado Springs, CO: University of the Rockies Press.

Hovarth, A. O. (1995). The therapeutic relationship: From transference to alliance. *In Session, 1,* 7–17.

Husserl, E. (1962). *Ideas: General introduction to pure pheneomenology* (W. R. Boyce Gibson, Trans.). New York: Collier. (Originally published 1913)

James, W. (1936). *The varieties of religious experience.* New York: Modern Library. (Original work published 1902)

Jamison, K. R. (1993). *Touched with fire: Manic-depressive illness and the artistic temperament.* New York: Free Press.

Jung, C. G. (1966). *Two essays on analytical psychology* (R. F. C. Hull, Trans.). Princeton, NJ: Princeton University Press.

Kierkegaard, S. (1944). *The concept of dread* (W. Lowrie, Trans.). Princeton, NJ: Princeton University Press. (Originally published 1844)

Krippner, S., & Paulson, D. (2007). *Haunted by combat: Understanding PTSD in war veterans, including women, reservists, and those coming back from Iraq.* Westport, CT: Greenwood.

Krug, O. T. (2009). James Bugental and Irvin Yalom: Two masters of existential therapy cultivate presence in the therapeutic encounter. *Journal of Humanistic Psychology, 49,* (3) Summer.

Krug, O. T., & Goulet, V. N. (2009). *The courage to change and become: Self-creation and therapeutic change as understood by Alfred N. Whitehead and Rollo May.* Unpublished manuscript.

Kuhl, V. (1994). The managed care revolution: Implications for humanistic psychotherapy. *Journal of Humanistic Psychology, 34,* 62–81.

Laing, R. D. (1967). *The politics of experience.* New York: Ballantine.

Laing, R. D. (Speaker). (1985). *Theoretical and practical aspects of existential therapy* (Cassette Recording No. L330-W1A). Phoenix, AZ: The Evolution of Psychotherapy conference, sponsored by the Erickson Institute.

Lambert, M. J. (1992). Implications of outcome research for psychotherapy integration. In J. C. Norcross & M. R. Goldstein (Eds.), *Handbook of psychotherapy integration.* New York: Basic Books.

Leijssen, M. (2006). Validation of the body in psychotherapy. *Journal of Humanistic Psychology, 46,* 126–146.

Lerner, M. (2000). *Spirit matters.* Charlottesville, VA: Hampton Roads.

Linley, P., & Joseph, S. (2007). Therapy work and therapists' positive and negative well-being. *Journal of Social and Clinical Psychology, 26,* 385–403.

Lyons, A. (2001). Humanistic psychology and social action. In K. J. Schneider, J. F. T. Bugental, & J. F. Pierson (Eds.), *The handbook of humanistic psychology: Leading edges in theory, practice, and research* (pp. 625–634). Thousand Oaks, CA: Sage.

Mahoney, M., & Mahoney, S. (2001). Living within essential tensions: Dialectics and future development. In K. Schneider et al. (Eds.), *The handbook of humanistic psychology* (pp. 659–665). Thousand Oaks: Sage Publications.

Mahrer, A. R. (1996). *The complete guide to experiential psychotherapy.* New York: Wiley.

Marcel, G. (1951). *Mystery of being—faith and reality.* Chicago: Gateway Edition.

Marcel, G. (1956). *The philosophy of existentialism.* New York: Philosophical Library.

May, R. (1958a). The origins and significance of the existential movement in psychology. In R. May, E. Angel, & H. Ellenberger (Eds.), *Existence* (pp. 3–36). New York: Basic Books.

May, R. (1958b). Contributions of existential psychotherapy. In R. May, E. Angel, & H. Ellenberger (Eds.), *Existence* (pp. 37–91). New York: Basic Books.

May, R. (1969). *Love and will.* New York: Norton.

May, R. (1972). *Power and innocence.* New York: Norton.

May, R. (1975). *The courage to create.* New York: Norton.

May, R. (1981). *Freedom and destiny.* New York: Norton.

May, R. (1983). *The discovery of being.* New York: Norton.

May, R. (Speaker). (2007). *Rollo May on existential psychotherapy* [DVD]. San Francisco: Psychotherapy.net.

May, R., & Yalom, I. (1995). Existential psychotherapy. In R. Corsini & D. Wedding (Eds.), *Current psychotherapies* (5th ed., pp. 262–292). Itasca, IL: Peacock.

Mendelowitz, E. (2001). Fellini, Fred, and Ginger: Imagology in a postmodern world. In K. J. Schneider, J. F. T. Bugental, & J. F. Pierson (Eds.), *The handbook of humanistic psychology: Leading edges in theory, practice, and research* (pp. 153–159). Thousand Oaks, CA: Sage.

Mendelowitz, E. (2008). *Lao Tzu and ethics: Intimations on character.* Colorado Springs, CO: University of the Rockies Press.

Mendelowitz, E., & Schneider, K. (2008). Existential psychotherapy. In R. Corsini & D. Wedding (Eds.), *Current psychotherapies* (8th ed., pp. 295–327). Belmont, CA: Thompson/Brooks/Cole.

Merleau-Ponty, M. (1962). *The phenomenology of perception* (C. Smith, Trans.). London: Routledge & Kegan Paul.

Messer, S. B., & Wampold, B. E. (2002). Let's face facts, common factors are more potent than specific therapy ingredients. *Clinical psychology: Science and practice, 9*(1), 21–25.

Miller, I. J. (1996a). Managed care is harmful to outpatient mental health services: A call for accountability. *Professional Psychology: Research and Practice, 27,* 349–363.

Miller, I. J. (1996b). Time-limited brief therapy has gone too far: The result is invisible rationing. *Professional Psychology: Research and Practice, 27,* 567–576.

Mitchell, S. (Trans.). (1988). *Tao te ching.* New York: Harper Collins. (Originally written by Lao Tzu, n.d.)

Monheit, J. (2008). A lesbian and gay perspective: The case of Marcia. In K. J. Schneider (Ed.), *Existential–integrative psychotherapy: Guideposts to the core of practice* (pp. 140–146). New York: Routledge.

Montuori, M., & Purser, R. (2001). Humanistic psychology and the workplace. In K. J. Schneider, J. F. T. Bugental, & J. F. Pierson (Eds.), *The handbook of humanistic psychology: Leading edges in theory, practice, and research* (pp. 635–644). Thousand Oaks, CA: Sage.

Mosher, L. (2001). Treating madness without hospitals: Soteria and its successors. In K. J. Schneider, J. F. T. Bugental, & J. F. Pierson (Eds.), *The handbook of humanistic psychology: Leading edges in theory, practice, and research* (pp. 389–402). Thousand Oaks, CA: Sage.

Moss, D. (Ed.). (1999*). Humanistic and transpersonal psychology: A historical and biographical sourcebook.* Westport, CT: Greenwood Press.

Moss, D. (2001). The roots and genealogy of humanistic psychology. In K. J. Schneider, J. F. T. Bugental, & J. F. Pierson (Eds.), *The handbook of humanistic psychology: Leading edges in theory, practice, and research* (pp. 5–20). Thousand Oaks, CA: Sage.

Moustakas, C. (1972). *Loneliness and love.* Englewood Cliffs, NJ: Prentice Hall.

Murray, H. A., Barret, W. G., Langer, W. C., Morgan, C. D., Homburger, E., et al. (1938). *Explorations in personality.* New York: Oxford University Press.

Nietzsche, F. (1982). Twilight of the idols. In W. Kaufmann (Ed.), *The portable Nietzche* (pp. 465–563). New York: Penguin. (Originally published 1889)

Norcross, J. (1987). A rational and empirical analysis of existential psychotherapy. *Journal of Humanistic Psychology, 27*(1), 41–68.

Norcross, J. C. (Ed.). (2002). *Psychotherapy relationships that work.* Oxford, England: Oxford University Press.

O'Hara, M. (2001). Emancipatory therapeutic practice for a new era: A work of retrieval. In K. J. Schneider, J. F. T. Bugental, & J. F. Pierson (Eds.), *The hand-*

book of humanistic psychology: Leading edges in theory, practice, and research (pp. 473–489). Thousand Oaks, CA: Sage.

Orlinsky, D. E., Grawe, K., & Parks, B. K. (1994). Process and outcome in psychotherapy—noch einmal. In A. E. Bergin & S. L. Garfield (Eds), *Handbook of psychotherapy and behavior change* (pp. 270–378). New York: Wiley.

Paulson, D. (2008). Wilber's integral philosophy: A summary and critique. *Journal of Humanistic Psychology, 48,* 364–388.

Penzel, F. (2000). *Obsessive-compulsive disorders: A complete guide to getting well and staying well.* Oxford, England: Oxford University Press.

Perls, F. (1971). *Gestalt therapy verbatim.* New York: Bantam Books.

Phillips, J. (1980–1981). Transference and encounter: The therapeutic relationship in psychoanalytic and existential therapy. *Review of Existential Psychology and Psychiatry, 17*(2/3), 135–152.

Pierson, J. F., & Sharp, J. (2001). Cultivating psychotherapist artistry: A model existential–humanistic training program. In K. J. Schneider, J. F. T. Bugental, & J. F. Pierson (Eds.), *The handbook of humanistic psychology: Leading edges in theory, practice, and research* (pp. 539–554). Thousand Oaks, CA: Sage.

Portnoy, D. (2008). Relatedness: Where existential and psychoanalytic psychotherapy converge. In K. J. Schneider (Ed.), *Existential–integrative psychotherapy: Guideposts to the core of practice* (pp. 268–281). New York: Routledge.

Rank, O. (1936). *Will therapy* (J. Taft, Trans.). New York: Knopf.

Ray, P. (1996, Spring). The rise of integral culture. *Noetic Sciences Review,* 4–15.

Rennie, D. L. (1994). Storytelling in psychotherapy: The client's subjective experience. *Psychotherapy, 31,* 234–243.

Rennie, D. L. (2002). Experiencing psychotherapy: Grounded theory studies. In D. J. Cain & J. Seeman (Eds.), *Humanistic psychotherapies: Handbook of research and practice* (pp. 117–144). Washington, DC: American Psychological Association.

Rescher, N. (2000). *Process philosophy: A survey of basic ideas.* Pittsburgh, PA: University of Pittsburgh Press.

Rice, D. (2008). An African American perspective: The case of Darrin. In K. J. Schneider (Ed.), *Existential–integrative psychotherapy: Guideposts to the core of practice* (pp. 110–121). New York: Routledge.

Richards, R. (1990). Everyday creativity, eminent creativity, and health: "Afterview" for Creativity Research Journal special issues on creativity and health. *Creativity Research Journal, 3,* 300–326.

Rogers, C. R. (1951). *Client-centered therapy: Its current practice, implications, and theory.* Boston: Houghton Mifflin.

Rowan, J. (2001). Existential analysis and humanistic psychotherapy. In K. J. Schneider, J. F. T. Bugental, & J. F. Pierson (Eds.), *The handbook of humanistic psychology: Leading edges in theory, practice, and research* (pp. 447–464). Thousand Oaks, CA: Sage.

Sartre, J. P. (1956). *Being and nothingness* (H. Barnes, Trans.). New York: Philosophical Library.

Schneider, K. J. (1985). Clients' perceptions of the positive and negative characteristics of their counselors. *Dissertation Abstracts International, 45*(10), 3345b. (University Microfilms International No. NN84217).

Schneider, K. J. (1993). *Horror and the holy: Wisdom-teachings of the monster tale.* Chicago: Open Court.

Schneider, K. J. (1995). Guidelines for an existential–integrative (EI) approach. In K. J. Schneider & R. May (Eds.), *The psychology of existence: An integrative, clinical perspective* (pp. 135–184). New York: McGraw-Hill.

Schneider, K. J. (1998a). Toward a science of the heart: Romanticism and the revival of psychology. *American Psychologist, 53,* 277–289.

Schneider, K. J. (1998b). Existential processes. In L. S. Greenberg, J. C. Watson, & G. Lietaer (Eds.), *Handbook of experiential psychotherapy* (pp. 103–120). New York: Guilford Press.

Schneider, K. J. (1999a). *The paradoxical self: Toward an understanding of our contradictory nature* (2nd ed.). Amherst, NY: Humanity Books

Schneider, K. J. (1999b). Clients deserve relationships, not merely "treatments." *American Psychologist, 54,* 206–207.

Schneider, K. J. (2001). Closing statement. In K. J. Schneider, J. F. T. Bugental, & J. F. Pierson (Eds.), *The handbook of humanistic psychology: Leading edges in theory, practice, and research* (pp. 672–675). Thousand Oaks, CA: Sage.

Schneider, K. J. (2004). *Rediscovery of awe: Splendor, mystery, and the fluid center of life.* St. Paul, MN: Paragon House.

Schneider, K. J. (2005). Biology and awe: Psychology's critical juncture. *Humanistic Psychologist, 33,* 167–173.

Schneider, K. J. (2007). The experiential liberation strategy of the existential–integrative model of therapy. *Journal of Contemporary Psychotherapy, 37,* 33–39.

Schneider, K. J. (2008). *Existential–integrative psychotherapy: Guideposts to the core of practice.* New York: Routledge.

Schneider, K. J. (2009). *Awakening to awe: Personal stories of profound transformation.* Lanham, MD: Jason Aronson.

Schneider, K. J., Bugental, J. F. T., & Pierson, J. (Eds.). (2001). *The handbook of humanistic psychology: Leading edges in theory, practice, and research.* Thousand Oaks, CA: Sage.

Schneider, K. J., & May, R. (Eds.). (1995). *The psychology of existence: An integrative, clinical perspective.* New York: McGraw-Hill.

Seligman, M. E. P. (1996). Science as an ally of practice. *American Psychologist, 51,* 1072–1079.

Serlin, I. A. (1996). Kinesthetic imagining. *Journal of Humanistic Psychology, 36*(2), 25–34.

Serlin, I. A. (Ed.). (2007). *Whole person healthcare,* Vols. 1–3. Westport, CT: Praeger.

Serlin, I. A. (2008). Women and the midlife crisis: The Anne Sexton complex. In K. J. Schneider (Ed.), *Existential–integrative psychotherapy: Guideposts to the core of practice* (pp. 146–163). New York: Routledge.

Serlin, I. A., & Marcow Speiser, V. (2007). Introduction to the special issue "Imagine: Expression in the service of humanity. *Journal of Humanistic Psychology, 47,* 280–287.

Shapiro, F. (1998). *EMDR: The breakthrough therapy for overcoming anxiety, stress and trauma.* New York: Basic Books.

Shedler, J., Mayman, M., & Manis, M. (1993). The illusion of mental health. *American Psychologist, 48,* 1117–1131.

Spinelli, E. (1997). *Tales of unknowing: Therapeutic encounters from an existential perspective.* London: Duckworth.

Spinelli, E. (2001). A reply to John Rowan. In K. J. Schneider, J. F. T. Bugental, & J. F. Pierson (Eds.), *The handbook of humanistic psychology: Leading edges in theory, practice, and research* (pp. 465–471). Thousand Oaks, CA: Sage.

Sterling, M. (2001). Expanding the boundaries of practice. In K. J. Schneider, J. F. T. Bugental, & J. F. Pierson (Eds.), *The handbook of humanistic psychology: Leading edges in theory, practice, and research* (pp. 349–353). Thousand Oaks, CA: Sage.

Stolorow, R. D. (2008). Autobiographical and theoretical reflections on the "ontological unconscious." In K. J. Schneider (Ed.), *Existential–integrative psychotherapy: Guideposts to the core of practice* (pp. 281–290). New York: Routledge.

Stolorow, R. D., Brandschaft, B., & Atwood, G. E. (1987). *Psychoanalytic treatment: An intersubjective approach.* Hillsdale, NJ: Analytic Press.

Sullivan, H. S. (1953). *The interpersonal theory of psychiatry.* New York: Norton.

Taylor, E. T. (1999). An intellectual renaissance in humanistic psychology? *Journal of Humanistic Psychology, 39*(2), 7–25.

Taylor, F. W. (1911). *Shop management, the principles of scientific management and testimony before the special house committee.* New York: Harper & Row.

Tillich, P. (1952). *The courage to be.* New Haven, CT: Yale University Press.

Thompson, M. G. (1995). Psychotic clients, Laing's treatment philosophy, and the fidelity to experience in existential psychoanalysis. In K. J. Schneider & R. May (Eds.), *The psychology of existence: An integrative, clinical perspective* (pp. 233–247). New York: McGraw-Hill.

Vontress, C. E., & Epp, L. R. (2001). Existential cross-cultural counseling: When hearts and cultures share. In K. J. Schneider, J. F. T. Bugental, & J. F. Pierson (Eds.), *The handbook of humanistic psychology: Leading edges in theory, practice, and research* (pp. 371–387). Thousand Oaks, CA: Sage.

Walsh, R. A., & McElwain, B. (2002). Existential psychotherapies. In D. J. Cain & J. Seeman (Eds.), *Humanistic psychotherapies: Handbook of research and practice* (pp. 253–278). Washington, DC: American Psychological Association.

Wampold, B. E. (2001). *The great psychotherapy debate: Models, methods, and findings.* Mahwah, NJ: Erlbaum.

Wampold, B. (2008, February 6). Existential-integrative psychotherapy comes of age. [Review of the book *Existential–integrative psychotherapy: Guideposts to the core of practice*]. *PsycCritiques 53,* Release 6, Article 1.

Watson, J. C., & Bohart, A. C. (2001). Humanistic-experiential therapies in the era of managed care. In K. J. Schneider, J. F. T. Bugental, & J. F. Pierson (Eds.), *The handbook of humanistic psychology: Leading edges in theory, practice, and research* (pp. 503–517). Thousand Oaks, CA: Sage.

Watson, J. C., & Rennie, D. L. (1994). Qualitative analysis of clients' subjective experience of significant moments during the exploration of problematic experiences. *Journal of Counseling Psychology, 41,* 500–509.

Welwood, J. (2001). The unfolding of experience: Psychotherapy and beyond. In K. J. Schneider, J. F. T. Bugental, & J. F. Pierson (Eds.), *The handbook of humanistic psychology: Leading edges in theory, practice, and research* (pp. 333–341). Thousand Oaks, CA: Sage.

Wertz, F. J. (2001). Humanistic psychology and the qualitative research tradition. In K. J. Schneider, J. F. T. Bugental, & J. F. Pierson (Eds.), *The handbook of humanistic psychology: Leading edges in theory, practice, and research* (pp. 231–245). Thousand Oaks, CA: Sage.

Westen, D., & Morrison, K. (2001). A multidimensional meta-analysis of treatments for depression, panic, and generalized anxiety disorder: An empirical examination of the status of empirically supported theories. *Journal of Consulting and Clinical Psychology, 69,* 875–899.

Westen, D., Novotny, C. M., & Thompson-Brenner, H. (2004). Empirical status of empirically supported psychotherapies: Assumptions, findings and reporting in controlled, clinical trials. *Psychological Bulletin, 130,* 631–663.

Wheelis, A. (1958). *The quest for existential identity.* New York: Norton.

Wolfe, B. (2008). Existential issues in anxiety disorders and their treatment. In K. J. Schneider (Ed.), *Existential–integrative psychotherapy: Guideposts to the core of practice* (pp. 204–216). New York: Routledge.

Wolpe, J. (1969). *The practice of behavior therapy.* New York: Pergamon.

Yalom, I. (1980*). Existential psychotherapy.* New York: Basic Books.

Yalom, I. (1989). *Love's executioner.* New York: Basic Books.

Yalom, I. (1998). *The Yalom reader.* New York: Basic Books.

Yalom, I. (2002). *The gift of therapy.* New York: HarperCollins.

Index

About the Authors

Kirk J. Schneider, PhD, is a licensed psychologist and leading spokesperson for contemporary humanistic psychology. He is current editor of the *Journal of Humanistic Psychology*, vice-president of the Existential–Humanistic Institute, and an adjunct faculty member at Saybrook Graduate School and the California Institute of Integral Studies in San Francisco. He is also a fellow of the American Psychological Association. Dr. Schneider has published over 100 articles and chapters and has authored or edited eight books, *The Paradoxical Self: Toward an Understanding of Our Contradictory Nature; Horror and the Holy: Wisdom-Teachings of the Monster Tale; The Psychology of Existence: An Integrative, Clinical Perspective* (with Rollo May; currently being translated into Chinese); *The Handbook of Humanistic Psychology: Leading Edges in Theory, Research, and Practice* (with J. Bugental and J. F. Pierson); *Rediscovery of Awe: Splendor, Mystery, and the Fluid Center of Life; Existential–Integrative Psychotherapy: Guideposts to the Core of Practice* (Chapter 5 currently being translated into Russian); and *Awakening to Awe: Personal Stories of Profound Transformation*. Most recently, Dr. Schneider coauthored with Ed Mendelowitz the chapter on Existential Psychotherapy for Corsini and Wedding's *Current Psychotherapies* (8th ed.). Dr. Schneider is the 2004 recipient of the Rollo May Award for "outstanding and independent pursuit of new frontiers in humanistic psychology" from Division 32 (Humanistic Psychology) of the American Psychological Association and the 2009 Cultural Innovator Award from the Living Institute of Toronto, Canada. In March 2010, Dr. Schneider is slated to deliver the keynote speech at the first East–West Existential Psychology Conference in Nanjing, China.

For further information about Dr. Schneider, visit his Web site at http://www.kirkjschneider.com.

Orah T. Krug, PhD, is a licensed psychotherapist with a private practice in Oakland, CA. She is the clinical training director of the Existential–Humanistic Institute of San Francisco and teaches at Saybrook Graduate School. Dr. Krug received her PhD from Saybrook Graduate School where she was awarded the Rollo May Scholarship for an essay comparing the theoretical approaches of her two mentors, James Bugental and Irvin Yalom. She has produced two videos, *Conversations With Jim* and *"Joe": A Demonstration of the Consultation Process, with James Bugental and Orah Krug.* Her current research focuses on the relationship between the cultivation of intra- and interpersonal presence and the contextual factors of therapy associated with therapeutic change. Her article in the *Journal of Humanistic Psychotherapy,* "James Bugental and Irvin Yalom, Two Masters of Existential Therapy Cultivate Presence," begins an exploration of this research. Dr. Krug may be reached at orahkrug@sbcglobal.net.